PTSD Solutions:

Achieve Emotional Stability by Managing Trauma Induced Anxiety Disorders, Depression, Stress, Flashbacks, Triggers, and Insomnia Using EMDR, CBT, and Holistic Modalities

Danielle Pataky

Table of Contents

Introduction

Healing takes courage, and we all have courage, even if we have to dig a little to find it. –Tori Amos

Post-traumatic stress disorder, also known as PTSD, is a disorder that is far more common than you think. Thousands of people suffer from PTSD in the United States alone, and what's worse is that many people have the wrong impression of what PTSD truly is. For example, many people still believe that only veterans can suffer from PTSD; however, that is not the case at all. When it comes to PTSD, anyone who has experienced something traumatic has the potential to suffer from it. Childhood abuse, abusive relationships, sexual abuse, workforce mistreatment, and more are all potential sources of developing PTSD, and that's not even all of the reasons one could develop such a harrowing disorder.

You might know that you are feeling the effects of PTSD, or you are curious about if it's something that you could possibly be suffering from. You might suffer from anxiety, insomnia, depression, and more as a result of your PTSD. You might have received a PTSD diagnosis and not know what it entails, or you are looking to learn more about how to overcome this disorder. Perhaps you're just here to support a loved one on their journey. Whatever your reason may be for joining me here today, I can help.

And why am I the right person to help you? Let me tell you a bit about my personal struggles with PTSD. My struggles with PTSD can be traced back to my childhood. I was not necessarily bullied, but "excluded" is a better term for the scenarios that I did face. I grew up in an environment where the predominant religion differed from my own, making me feel dirty and unmatched–the customs and rules were unfamiliar, and my experiences in people's homes were not too kind to say the least. These early childhood experiences set the tone for the rest of my life. As we progress through the book, you will hear more details about my personal struggle, hopefully allowing you to feel like you are less alone in the battle.

So, while I'm not a mental health professional, I know a thing or two about overcoming the grips of PTSD because I've experienced it first-hand. Throughout this all new, just for you book about overcoming PTSD, you will learn about the impact of the disorder, how to treat it yourself using holistic methods, and much more. By the end of this book, I promise you will feel far more equipped to handle the struggles associated with PTSD. You'll be able to live a life that is inspired by healing, one where your past is a part of you and not your whole life.

PTSD may not have a cure, but it does have associated tools to ease the struggles you feel. I firmly believe that you have what it takes to overcome the grip your PTSD has on your life, especially if you employ the tools presented in this book.

So, without a second of further delay, let's get started with your journey into a new life—I know you have what it takes to empower yourself on this journey.

Chapter 1:
Understanding PTSD

Trauma is personal. It does not disappear if it is not validated. When it is ignored or invalidated the silent screams continue internally heard only by the one held captive. When someone enters the pain and hears the screams, healing can begin. —Danielle Bernock

PTSD, also known as post-traumatic stress disorder, is incredibly complex. Many people seem to think that they know what it entails, but there are a lot of misconceptions and wrongful beliefs about the disorder. Even if you yourself have PTSD, it may be the case that you do not know how to succinctly define the condition nor what constitutes it. Over the course of the next few pages, I'll teach you all about PTSD—what it is, what it entails, how to dispel some of the most common myths that surround PTSD, and more.

Definition of PTSD and Symptoms

PTSD is a disorder characterized by the fact that, in order to develop the disorder, one must have experienced something traumatic. While the condition was first recognized among war veterans—which contributes to the misleading idea that only veterans have the condition—it is now recognized that PTSD can be caused by a diverse set of experiences. Just a few of the potential causes of PTSD include (Mind, 2021a):

- experiencing a car accident.

- being subjected to rape or sexual assault.

- enduring abuse, harassment, or bullying related to your identity, including racism, sexism, homophobia, biphobia, or transphobia.

- encountering a situation where your life is at risk, such as being kidnapped or held hostage.

- going through a violent incident, whether it is military combat, a terrorist attack, or any form of assault.

- witnessing others being harmed or killed, including in the context

- working in a profession where you regularly witness or hear distressing events, like the emergency services or armed forces.

- surviving a natural disaster, such as flooding, earthquakes, or pandemics like the coronavirus pandemic.

- experiencing a traumatic childbirth as a mother or witnessing a traumatic birth as a partner.

- losing someone close to you under particularly distressing circumstances.

- being involuntarily committed or receiving treatment in a mental health facility.

- receiving a diagnosis of a life-threatening illness.

As you can see, PTSD has no limitations on the breadth of trauma that you have to face in order to be diagnosed with PTSD. There is also something called complex PTSD, abbreviated as C-PTSD. C-PTSD involves experiencing PTSD along with some additional symptoms, which we will talk about later on. Treating PTSD and C-PTSD is a very similar process, but understanding how the condition manifests within yourself is vital to the recovery process.

So, what are the symptoms involved in PTSD? Generally, the symptoms of PTSD can be broken into three categories: re-experiencing symptoms, avoidance symptoms, and hyperarousal symptoms (NHS, 2021).

Re-experiencing symptoms

Re-experiencing symptoms are the most common symptoms that someone with PTSD will experience. These symptoms involve an involuntary reliving of a traumatic event, including things like flashbacks or nightmares, distressing sensations, and physical sensations reminiscent of the traumatic event. In addition, with re-experiencing symptoms, someone may repeatedly have negative thoughts concerning the event, as well as thoughts that prevent themselves from coming to terms with the event. In general, re-experiencing symptoms are what most people think about when it comes to PTSD–reliving the traumatic event.

Avoidance Symptoms

Next, there are avoidance symptoms. Avoidance symptoms will involve someone with PTSD trying their hardest to avoid reminders of the event that traumatized them. For most people who experience avoidance symptoms, this will include avoiding people and places that remind them of their trauma. In a lot of cases, someone will try to force these memories out of their brain or will try to not feel anything at all–also referred to as emotional numbing. As a result, someone who engages in avoidance may become isolated and depressed in order to avoid remembering their traumatic experiences.

Hyperarousal Symptoms

There also exists something referred to as hyperarousal symptoms. Hyperarousal, especially in PTSD, describes a state wherein someone is consistently very anxious and cannot relax, as they're constantly on guard for potential threats. This can cause someone to be especially prone to irritability and anger, trouble getting enough sleep, and a difficulty when it comes to remaining focused.

Symptoms of C-PTSD

Finally, I wanted to touch briefly on some of the common symptoms of C-PTSD. As I mentioned, C-PTSD involves all of the symptoms of PTSD with the addition of symptoms such as (Mind, 2021b):

- difficulty controlling your emotions.

- feeling very angry or distrustful towards the world.

- constant feelings of emptiness or hopelessness.

- feeling as if you are permanently damaged or worthless.

- feeling as if you are completely different to other people.

- feeling like nobody can understand what happened to you.

- avoiding friendships and relationships, or finding them very difficult.

- often experiencing dissociative symptoms such as

depersonalisation or derealisation.

- physical symptoms, such as headaches, dizziness, chest pains and stomach aches.

- regular suicidal feelings.

Causes and Risk Factors

When it comes to any mental disorder, there are many causes and risk factors that can increase the potential for someone to develop that disorder. PTSD is no different. While it is necessary for a traumatic event to have occurred for someone to have PTSD, biological factors can increase how prone someone is to develop this disorder. Let's explore the causes and risk factors involved in someone developing PTSD together.

Traumatic Events

Traumatic events are the first major cause and risk factor for PTSD. While it only takes one traumatic event for someone to develop the condition, someone who has repeatedly faced trauma over and over again is more likely to develop PTSD due to the repeated and compounding trauma. And as mentioned earlier, trauma is not confined to one thing–trauma can be anything from COVID-19 experiences to severe abuse, and the traumatic event and its severity plays no role on the severity of someone's PTSD. Everyone is an individual, and as such everyone responds differently to trauma.

Biological Factors

In addition to trauma-based sources for your PTSD, there may be genetic or biological predispositions that make you more likely to develop PTSD. It is not a disorder that is passed down traditionally, however. There is not a PTSD gene necessarily, nor is it passed down via environmental or physical bodily factors that one experiences at birth. Rather, some researchers seem to believe that PTSD and trauma more generally are passed down because these events leave a "mark" on the genes of our parents, which gets passed down to us (Can We Inherit PTSD from Our Parents? | Genetics and Genomics, n.d.). In other words, if one of your parents has experienced some form of trauma, recent studies indicate that this can make you more susceptible to developing trauma of your own due to the impact this has on your parents' lives directly.

Diagnosing PTSD

It might come as a surprise to you, but not everyone who faces trauma will develop PTSD. Some people walk out unscathed entirely, making it necessary for certain diagnostic criteria to be present for the diagnosis of PTSD to take place. In other words, PTSD isn't diagnosed on the mere presence of trauma alone—it relies on myriad other symptoms to be considered present. Please note that this is not an attempt to diagnose you with anything; I am not a doctor and cannot do that. Rather, use this section as encouragement to seek professional help if you think that you might have PTSD based on common symptoms and experiences of the disorder.

Criteria for Diagnosing

When you go to a doctor who can diagnose you with PTSD, there are a few things that they will look for. In general, doctors follow something called the Diagnostic and Statistical Manual: 5th Edition for the most current rules on diagnoses, which is also called the DSM-V. This is a manual containing every mental illness and disorder that we know of, as well as its diagnostic criteria. Referencing the DSM-V is how any mental diagnosis is made and has been made throughout recent history. According to the DSM-V, which is developed through decades of research and study, there are a few criteria that someone must meet in order to be diagnosed with PTSD.

For PTSD, there are eight criteria one must meet in order to be diagnosed, with each criteria labeled A through H. For example, for criteria A, someone has encountered actual or threatened death, violence, or serious injury either via direct exposure, witnessing the trauma, learning about someone close experiencing the trauma, or via indirect exposure (as a first responder may endure, for instance) (Brainline, 2018). If none of that is true, then you cannot be diagnosed with PTSD. Each of the following seven criteria are similar:

- Criteria B: The trauma one experienced must be persistent in how it is re-experienced, in one or more of the following ways: nightmares, unwanted and upsetting memories, flashbacks, emotional distress after reminders of the trauma, physical distress after reminders of the trauma.

- Criteria C: Someone must have an avoidance symptom pertaining to their trauma, either in ignoring thoughts and feelings of the event or in ignoring external reminders.

- Criteria D: In addition, someone must experience negative feelings or thoughts that got worse as a result of the trauma, including being unable to recall parts of the trauma, being overly negative about oneself or the world, blaming themselves or others for the trauma, experiencing a decreased interest in former activities of interest, feelings of isolation, and difficulty experiencing positive emotions.

- Criteria E: Moreover, a PTSD sufferer will experience arousal and reactivity that gets worse as a result of the trauma, including irritability, destructive or impulsive behavior, hypervigilance, and difficulty focusing or sleeping.

- Criteria F: Symptoms must be persistent for more than one month to qualify as PTSD.

- Criteria G: The trauma must cause significant impairment or disturbance in daily life.

- Criteria H: These symptoms must not be due to medication, substance abuse, or another mental health condition.

If someone fits into all eight of those criteria, then a doctor will diagnose them with PTSD. This means that if you experience all eight of those criteria but do not have a PTSD diagnosis, then it may be in your best interest to consult with a psychiatrist about potential evaluation.

Dispelling Misconceptions about PTSD

PTSD is just one of hundreds of mental disorders with misconceptions, stigma, and misunderstanding surrounding its very essence. As you progress through your journey, you yourself or others around you may hold misconstrued beliefs about what PTSD is and what it means to have the disorder. Dedicating a few moments to learning about the most common misconceptions surrounding PTSD can minimize some of the struggles that you may face within recovery.

The first big misconception is that PTSD only impacts those who are or were in the military in some capacity. This is blatantly untrue, as you have probably learned by now. Any form of trauma, big or small and regardless of the circumstance, can cause PTSD. The misconception that only veterans are able to have PTSD is one that is quite dangerous. The wrongful belief that only one group of people face a disorder causes many people who need and deserve help to avoid seeking it out. As such, it is crucial to dispel this myth.

In addition, it is untrue that everyone who experiences trauma will also experience PTSD. Trauma is necessary to have PTSD, but it does not necessitate the disorder. In other words, someone can experience something traumatic but not develop any mental health issues at all. This is because some people are naturally at greater risk of developing PTSD–it has nothing to do with how weak or strong someone is. If you have experienced repeated or multiple forms of trauma and grew up in an unsafe environment, then naturally you will be more likely to develop PTSD than someone who grew up in a safe environment and only ever had traumatic experiences with COVID, for example.

The final major myth that I want to dispel before we move forward is the idea that PTSD just goes away on its own. PTSD can be lessened or relieved, but typically only after seeking medical and professional help to overcome that trauma. Just ignoring it and hoping it'll go away is the worst thing you can do–it both takes time away from recovery and allows that trauma to fester. Instead of hoping that your trauma will go away on its own, it is important to take proactive steps–as you are doing right now–to allow yourself to heal.

Exploring the Impact of Trauma on the Mind and Body and on Daily Life

One of the requirements for being diagnosed with PTSD is that the trauma you faced causes significant disturbance, disruption, or other impact on your daily life. Undoubtedly, if you have read this far and you are someone who has experienced trauma, it has impacted you in many ways–some of which you might not be aware of. Becoming aware of the impact that trauma can have on the mind and body is an important step forward. Doing so allows you to understand how your trauma has personally impacted you, as well as where you might want to begin in the recovery process.

Trauma has a handful of mental health effects that are common. For example, let's consider flashbacks. Flashbacks occur when you continue to relive a form of trauma over and over, feeling as though it is occurring again in real time. This is a way that trauma can impact your mind and your daily life, as flashbacks are no joke. Often, they can leave you just as shaken up as when the trauma first occurred, and a flashback can turn an ordinary day into one where nothing gets done at all due to the effects of trauma. You might also experience symptoms like panic attacks of dissociation as a result of your trauma and how it impacts the brain. Furthermore, sleep problems, hyperarousal, and low self-esteem often accompany PTSD mental health aspects as well.

But that's not all. Trauma can also impact your physical body. Studies have shown that people who experience trauma are more prone to developing chronic health conditions, like chronic pain or stress. Furthermore, stress on its own can impact the body in a lot of ways due to a surge in the hormone cortisol, which is associated with stress responses. When your body experiences a surplus of this hormone, it can cause issues for your heart, lungs, reproductive and digestive systems, etc., making it rather difficult to recover in a physical sense. Physical sensations can also find their way into your life as a result of your trauma. It is not uncommon for someone who has experienced trauma to physically feel as though they're reliving it again.

The Importance of Seeking Help for PTSD

A lot of people avoid seeking help for their PTSD. For a while, I was someone who avoided doing so too. However, by seeking help for your PTSD, you open up a world of opportunity for recovery, growth, and a new chance at life. While no amount of therapy or medication can revoke your trauma, it can help you become more acquainted with a new way of living that is friendlier and more compatible with who you are now. In fact, that's one of the goals of this book. By picking up this book, you are taking an important first step in trauma recovery, and I encourage you to continue to move forward in your journey. If, at any point, you think you'd benefit more highly from professional services, I implore you to seek them out–I am not a medical professional.

In this chapter, you learned all about what PTSD is, how it is diagnosed, and some of the misconceptions that surround it. This is helpful in beginning your journey with PTSD recovery, because it allows you to understand just what you are tackling when you begin the process. In the next chapter, you will learn all about the powers of eye movement desensitization reprocessing (EMDR) therapy for PTSD.

Chapter 2:
EMDR Therapy for PTSD

Not until we are lost do we begin to find ourselves. —Henry David Thoreau

There are many treatment options available when it comes to dealing with what PTSD can throw at you, and one of my favorites is EMDR therapy. EMDR therapy, otherwise known as eye movement desensitization reprocessing therapy, is one of the best and most effective manners for dealing with PTSD and other forms of trauma and mental health conditions. Together, let's dive into what EMDR is and how it can be used to help you in your recovery process.

What is EMDR Therapy?

Initially developed in the late 1980s, EMDR therapy was developed specifically to treat symptoms of post-traumatic stress disorder—such as flashbacks, nightmares, anxiety disorders, depression, stress, triggers, and more. It employs the Adaptive Information Processing model to provide individual therapy for six to twelve sessions in order to treat symptoms. EMDR involves utilizing natural patterns of eye movement to desensitize someone to an event that they experienced—most typically one of traumatic standing—and then reprocess the memory. This is based on the fundamental idea that trauma is relived through PTSD due to an inability for the brain to properly process the events that took place.

EMDR works by using something called bilateral stimulation. This involves a therapist working with you to engage both parts of the brain during rapid eye movement, and sessions usually last for an hour. The idea is that the bilateral stimulation process moves stuck memories to allow the left side of the brain to soothe the right one. In EMDR therapy, a patient is guided to reprocess memories in a way that allows them to feel a peaceful solution to something—especially in the event that they got no closure.

For example, let's say that someone got assaulted physically on their way out of their workplace, and then the attacker ran off. If this person wanted to try out EMDR therapy, the therapist would help them to reprocess the attack in a way that solidifies positive affirmations and positive resolution in their mind, convincing them that they got the closure they needed and can move on from the event once and for all. This doesn't mean, contrary to popular belief, that the victim is brainwashed out of thinking that their trauma occurred. Rather, this means that the memory of the trauma is reprocessed in a way that allows one to understand that the event is over and that they are now, as a result, safe.

The Adaptive Information Processing Model

Crucial to EMDR therapy is something called the Adaptive Information Processing model. What is this and how does it connect? This model proposes that we as humans process information that is stored in memory networks. When a memory is stored improperly, as is often the case with memories pertaining to trauma, it can cause information to be processed irrationally—resulting in triggers, anxiety, stress, fear, depression symptoms, and more. All of this occurs within the prefrontal cortex. This connects to EMDR because it is a fundamental principle explaining why it may work. The truth is that we do not know exactly why EMDR works, but thanks to the Adaptive Information Processing model, we're pretty sure that it works by reframing these poorly stored memories so that the brain can rationalize them.

Research on EMDR Therapy

As with anything in science, understanding the research that goes into something is an important aspect of being able to understand whether it is right for you. After all, you would not take a medicine that a doctor prescribed if they'd not looked into why it worked and the efficiency of it before giving it to you, right? Plus, it is good to know that they find that medicine to be the best for you given your circumstances. By exploring the efficacy and comparisons of EMDR therapy, you can determine if it is the right option for you.

The vast majority of research on EMDR therapy dictates that it is both effective in its own right and serves as a marvelous way to combat psychological trauma. For example, one study declared that as a result of randomized clinical trials, EMDR is effective for addressing both mental and physical symptoms that can arise as a result of trauma (Shapiro, 2014). Evidence also suggests that not only is EMDR effective, but it can also work faster than many other forms of therapy (EMDR Therapy: What It Is, Procedure & Effectiveness, n.d.).

As you embark upon your EMDR journey, there may be a question burning in the back of your mind: how does EMDR compare to other forms of therapy in terms of effectiveness? This is a question that a lot of people ask when it comes to trying out different forms of therapy. In fact, many people draw comparisons between EMDR and its cousin, cognitive behavioral therapy (CBT), which we will talk about in the next chapter. For now, let's focus on how EMDR compares to other forms of therapy that are used in the context of trauma.

First, let's compare it to CBT. A lot of people seeking out therapeutic benefits tend to question whether they should go for CBT or EMDR. In general, if you are going to try and remedy anxiety due to trauma or other symptoms that arise as a result of PTSD, then EMDR is going to be your best bet. EMDR has been noted to have a higher efficacy rate as far as reducing stress and anxiety in PTSD sufferers goes. Additionally, the vast majority of patients seem to appreciate EMDR more, stating that it was a better experience overall as compared to their CBT experiences.

EMDR can also be compared to dialectical behavioral therapy (DBT). In general, the more effective option here is going to depend on your personal goals for therapy. At its core, DBT serves to help a client develop coping skills that allow them to live with their trauma more easily. EMDR, on the other hand, directly seeks to alleviate symptoms rather than teaching skills. Therefore, depending on what you want out of therapy, DBT may be a more valuable option for you.

This book dedicates a chapter each to CBT and EMDR, but not DBT. Why is that? Simply put, it is because DBT focuses on skills, and most of the book aims to teach you skills that you can use to combat struggles pertaining to PTSD. In other words, this book does not exclude DBT at all; rather, it focuses on integrating it alongside EMDR and CBT in an effective capacity.

The EMDR Therapy Process

There are two different ways in which you can engage with EMDR therapy: with a professional, and alone. I recommend seeking out professional help where possible, but do not worry—I know that this is not the most accessible thing in the world, so the next section focuses on guiding yourself through the process of receiving EMDR therapy.

Assuming you elect to seek professional guidance for your EMDR journey, you might be wondering what to expect from an appointment or the process altogether. Generally speaking, the process of EMDR either with a professional or in your own home is similar; however, the steps that you will likely experience with a professional EMDR guide are as follows

(Experiencing EMDR Therapy, n.d.):

1. Phase 1: History and treatment planning. This phase will generally take at least one full session, and during this phase your therapist would work with you in order to develop a treatment plan that specifically targets a key event, present events that upset you, and skills that would help you. This is mostly an evaluative phase.

2. Phase 2: Preparation. This phase involves your therapist explaining EMDR to you as well as what you can expect during the process. Each therapist does things a bit differently, so it is important to pay attention as your therapist explains these things.

3. Phase 3: Assessment. This phase involves you identifying things that need to be processed during EMDR. You will determine what it is that needs to be worked on and reprocessed. You will also be asked to state how true you feel your beliefs to be, also known as Validity of Cognition. If you are only focusing on one thing during treatment, it may take about three sessions to reprocess the memory.

4. Phase 4: Desensitization. During this phase, you will focus on "reliving" your disturbing memory that you are trying to resolve. This will allow you to work on desensitizing yourself to the event using movement, sound, or taps in order to trick your brain.

5. Phase 5: Installation. This involves "installing" new, positive memories and thoughts that allow your brain to reprocess what occurred.

6. Phase 6: Body scan. This involves a body scan meditation that looks to see if there is any physical indication that trauma has been unresolved. Generally, your therapist will work to find tension within the body upon mentioning the target.

7. Phase 7: Closure. This involves ending the treatment session in a way that lets you feel more positive.

8. Phase 8: Reevaluation. At the beginning of each session, you and your therapist will discuss the progress you have made.

It might sound vague, but because each therapist performs EMDR differently, you will need to meet with them to understand their particular process. Although, generally your therapist will follow a pattern of asking you to look at a moving target while thinking about your trauma, and then repeat the same eye movement thinking about a positive outcome that gives you closure. While many people feel improvements after the first rapid eye movement session, for others it can take a few sessions for benefits to be experienced.

But what if you cannot afford to see a therapist to help you through the process? Let's talk about it.

Engaging in EMDR on Your Own: A Step-by-Step Guide

If you cannot afford to go to a professional for EMDR therapy, or do not feel comfortable doing so, there are still options for you. Many resources are available online to help individuals along with the process of EMDR therapy. Performing EMDR on yourself is possible, and can be carried out with the following steps:

1. Prepare for the experience. You should engage in EMDR when you feel mentally strong—it is not a good idea to go into this lightly, especially if you are self-administering the practice. Work on relaxing your mind and body beforehand, and find an appropriate time and place where you can engage with EMDR in the comfort of your own home.

2. Select an experience that you want to use for your EMDR practice. You can do so by thinking of something that makes you deeply upset, an event or thought process that is hindering you in life. Then, rate how severely the experience is impacting you out of 10.

3. Set a positive belief or goal for your practice—a first-person statement. For example, "I am safe" or "I am in control" are really good positive beliefs to select.

4. Bilateral stimulation is the next step, which involves engaging a pattern within your brain from the left side to the right side. Bilateral stimulation creates relaxation within the brain. For self-administered EMDR, you are going to need to pick a video that has a dot which moves back and forth across the screen. YouTube has hundreds of these videos, and I especially recommend blue dots due to their calming nature. Set the video up in full screen mode with headphones on for the best effect.

5. Start the video. Follow the dot with your eyes as you focus on your target memory or event, imagining it in as much detail as possible. You should feel at least somewhat uncomfortable, and you should let yourself stay in this space for about two minutes.

6. Take a five minute break where you do not think about anything, just focusing on your breathing.

7. Return to your video and imagine the positive statement as real as possible, just like you did with the negative event. Do this for two minutes, before moving to the next step.

8. Close your eyes. Imagine the event as though it has already come true and that you are living in your reality that is comforting and includes your healing thoughts.

9. Conduct a body scan meditation—which you can find on YouTube as well—and notice if tension lingers in your body. If it does, you will need to repeat the process again. If not, you are good to go.

In addition, I recommend taking a look at my EMDR and CBT workbook—[title]. In that workbook, you can find...

In this chapter, you have learned all about EMDR—including what it is, how it works, and how to perform it yourself at home. The next chapter focuses all on another method of therapy: cognitive behavioral therapy (CBT).

Chapter 3:
Cognitive Behavioral Therapy (CBT) for PTSD

I think that little by little I'll be able to solve my problems and survive.
—Frida Kahlo

Cognitive behavioral therapy, also known as CBT, is another method that is particularly effective for the treatment of PTSD. While CBT is typically experienced under the guidance of a professional, certain methods can also be employed by yourself in order to reap the most benefits from your practice and healing journey, especially if you cannot afford traditional therapies as is. We'll dive deeper into this in this chapter.

What is CBT?

CBT refers to a form of therapy called psychotherapy, which is a fancy word for talk therapy. CBT and its methods were developed by Aaron Beck in the 1960s. CBT is goal oriented, meaning that your psychiatrist (or yourself if you are doing this alone) would be responsible for helping you set a goal. By the end of your practice, you should achieve this goal, which means that it inherently has to be one that is realistic. CBT involves a few core principles, and understanding them is crucial to your successful employment of CBT (Cleveland Clinic, 2022):

- Psychological issues are partly caused by unhelpful or intrinsically problematic thinking patterns.

- Psychological issues are also caused in part by learned patterns of unhelpful or damaging behavior.

- Psychological issues are thirdly caused by problematic core beliefs about one's self and the world around them.

- Finally, those experiencing psychological issues can learn ways to cope with them and alleviate associated symptoms.

How Does it Work?

As mentioned, when you begin CBT, your therapist is going to encourage you to set a goal. An example of a strong CBT goal would be something like "I no longer respond by [behavior] when exposed to [trigger]." This is a good example because it works directly with a core principle of CBT and the methods that will be used. Namely, this goal works by allowing you to overcome something called cognitive distortions—flaws in thinking that cause us to think inaccurately or inappropriately based on a scenario—so that our thoughts become more grounded in logic and reason. Just a few of the cognitive distortions you may be familiar with in your own thinking include (Hartney, 2020)

- All or nothing thinking. This involves viewing situations in black and white rather than recognizing things within shades of gray. For example, let's say that you set a goal for yourself to completely clean your house in a day. Within that day, you do not get the house clean, but you do get some things crossed off your chore list. If you think with an all or nothing mindset, you are going to consider this a failure—you did not do it all, so you might as well have done nothing. But a more logical mindset dictates that you congratulate yourself for the progress you have made!

- Overgeneralization. Overgeneralization involves making a rule after experiencing something isolated. In other words, if you notice that when you went to the park for the first time, a thunderstorm suddenly moved in, making a rule that going to the park is bad luck is an overgeneralization. This does nothing but prevent you from going somewhere, because the rule is not based in reality; rather, it is based on an isolated, general event that could happen to anyone with any place.

- Discounting the positive. This cognitive distortion is exactly what it sounds like. Instead of acknowledging both positive and negative experiences in life, someone prone to discounting the positive is only going to discount positive experiences. For example, if you get a bonus at work for your hard work, discounting the positive might be thinking that you only got the bonus because you "tricked" your boss and that you did not actually do anything positive.

- Jumping to conclusions. Jumping to conclusions can involve two different cognitive distortions: mind reading and fortune telling. When someone engages in mindreading, they assume that someone is going to react a certain way or that they're thinking something they're not. Fortune telling involves predicting that events will unfold in a particular way rather than accept what's going to happen—a cognitive distortion that is commonly used when it comes to trying to avoid something difficult.

- Personalization. This involves taking an event that happened to you and making it about you, as if it were your fault or done specifically to wrong you.

As you and your therapist (or you and yourself) work through cognitive distortions like the ones I've mentioned, you will begin to notice marked changes in your behavior, thought processes, and responses to things around you. This methodology is at the core of how CBT works.

On Dialectical Behavioral Therapy

Dialectical behavioral therapy, also known as DBT, is a form of CBT that you might have heard about or be interested in trying. Some key facts to know about DBT include:

- It is a form of talk therapy that has been around since the 1980s.

- Primarily, DBT was intended to be used in the treatment of those with borderline personality disorder—BPD—but success has been observed when it comes to the employment of DBT for other mental health conditions.

- DBT bases itself on CBT principles, combining itself with mindfulness practices. Distress tolerance and emotional regulation is also covered.

If you think that DBT may be for you, I highly recommend discussing it with your primary care provider.

The CBT Therapy Process

When you undergo CBT, it is important to know that each practitioner does something a little bit different; however, there are still some commonalities that you can look forward to as things that are the same across most practices. This includes cognitive restructuring, exposure therapy, and skills training.

What is cognitive restructuring exactly? Cognitive restructuring is a CBT technique that alters the way you think. One of the fundamental principles of CBT is that our thoughts are flawed and that can cause mental health issues. By working with cognitive restructuring, you can overcome those aforementioned cognitive distortions. The process of cognitive restructuring is simple. It involves identifying a distressing situation and what leads to it, then evaluating how valid those thoughts are. This allows you to determine a new, more productive thought.

DIY Cognitive Restructuring

Cognitive restructuring is one of the easiest things that you can do in the comfort of your own home. As an example, I've created the following for you to observe how cognitive restructuring works:

Statement:	I am never going to be safe again.
Thoughts:	I'm not safe in my home, everyone's out to get me, and I'm never going to be safe ever again.
Feelings:	Scared, sad.
Evidence to the contrary:	My apartment door and windows have locks. No one has ever broken into my unit, nor has anyone followed me home. I have weapons hidden that I know how to use, and people have my location just in case something happens.
Supporting evidence:	None.
Balanced thought:	I may feel unsafe, but there are measures in place that are protecting me.

Now, do the same thing below with a thought of your own:

Statement:	

Thoughts:	
Feelings:	
Evidence to the contrary:	
Supporting evidence:	
Balanced thought:	

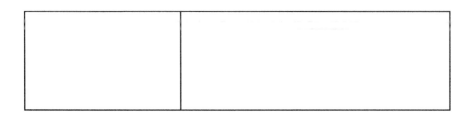

This is the simplest way to work with cognitive restructuring. It might be difficult at first. Something I struggled with when it came to CBT was truly believing those restructured thoughts. The secret is to repeat them to yourself until they become true; it might sound silly, but it really works!

Exposure Therapy

Another method that is commonly used to treat patients in cognitive behavioral therapy is exposure therapy. Exposure therapy is exactly what it sounds like—exposing a patient to something that can be triggering in order to give them exposure to it in a positive way. The intention of doing so is so that clients can engage with triggers in a more positive way. For example, someone who is undergoing exposure therapy for a phobia might be introduced to that phobia in small doses until it causes less fear. This is beneficial in CBT especially. This is because CBT states that we all have unconscious, automatic thoughts—thoughts that we do not know are happening, yet can affect our mood and motivations. As a result, exposing yourself to something that causes these automatic thoughts can help eliminate them.

At first, many people worry about the effectiveness of exposure therapy. Besides, is it not cruel to expose someone to something that they're afraid of or triggered by? Well, not necessarily. For starters, all exposure therapy is consensual, and the risks of it are disclosed to a patient prior to the beginning of the practice. Moreover, exposure therapy has demonstrated effectiveness time and time again, proving to be a wonderful method in improving symptoms in up to 90% of patients (Exposure Therapy for Anxiety: What to Expect and Effectiveness, 2021).

When you partake in exposure therapy with a professional—whether it be for PTSD, anxiety, or something else—there are a handful of things that you can always expect. There are different types of exposure therapy, and depending on the one that you are partaking in, you can expect something a bit different. The two main methods that people here about include (Exposure Therapy: What It Is and What to Expect, 2020):

- In vivo exposure therapy: During in vivo exposure therapy, a

22

patient is encouraged to work toward confronting a phobia. So, for example, if you are in exposure therapy due to a phobia of spiders, you may eventually work your way up to holding a spider without fear.

- Imaginal exposure therapy: Imaginal exposure therapy involves imagining a trigger or a situation in vivid detail, as this is the safest and most effective way to handle trauma. This is likely what you will experience in the next section as you guide yourself through exposure therapy.

Generally speaking, you should always seek professional guidance for exposure therapy in case it becomes too triggering. Not only does professional guidance help with this, but it allows you to manage pacing as well.

DIY Exposure Therapy

Experiencing exposure therapy with a professional is one thing, but not everyone has access to therapy in this manner. Because of this, here are some considerations if you want to undergo exposure therapy on your own:

- Before you begin, make sure that you are in a setting that is both safe and comfortable. You may want to have water and a light snack nearby, and make sure that you are not in a public setting either. I recommend doing this surrounded by pillows and blankets, but any place that brings you comfort is good.

- Start small. It might be tempting to jump right in with resolving all of your most significant traumas as soon as you begin your session, but I heavily recommend starting small and waiting a while before diving into bigger situations. Not only is exposure therapy triggering, but it is something that requires extensive amounts of practice. It is better to give yourself that time to practice before jumping into resolving larger traumas.

- Practice. Exposure therapy is like exercise; if you want it to work, you have to do it over and over until you are proficient at it. In order for imaginal exposure therapy to work, you have to be good at both visualizing and interacting with that visualization. Therefore, it is also a good idea to practice visualization techniques separate from exposure therapy.

- Know when you have reached your limits. The point of exposure therapy is to expose you to something that makes you uncomfortable, which is going to push your limits; however, you should not be sending yourself into unending panic attacks with your methods. Instead, when you feel you have had enough, stop— you can always go further next time!

Skills Training

Skills training is the third component of CBT. It involves learning skills that are lacking through modeling, instruction, and roleplay so that a patient can learn skills to cope with and navigate life. Some skills that CBT skills training can help you navigate include:

- Problem solving.

- Relaxation.

- Introspection.

- Conflict resolution.

- Journaling.

- Cognitive restructuring.

And more!

If you are looking for a solid arrangement of skills training worksheets, I recommend checking out the same workbook I mentioned in the EMDR section!

My Experience With CBT

I've had personal, up-close accounts of trauma that began as early as my childhood. I guess you can say I'm pretty experienced when it comes to not only trauma, but the accompanying solutions to it as well. One of the solutions that I tried was cognitive behavioral therapy, which is why I feel confident in recommending it to you. I want to tell you a bit about my experience with CBT before leading you off into the next chapter.

Originally, I was hesitant to dive into CBT—I had heard such mixed things about it, because I was trying it during a time where there was so much conflicting information. Still, my insurance covered it, so I was willing to give it a shot. After all, what could it hurt? I scheduled an appointment and went in for my first session, a bit afraid and unsure of what to think.

My therapist, over the course of about five or six sessions, asked me to set relevant goals and markers that would indicate success in our efforts. Throughout the sessions, she taught me about cognitive restructuring. I came to learn that a lot of the reasons I felt so trapped with my trauma came down to cognitive distortions—the way I was thinking held me back. It felt so moving and powerful to be able to move forward with her help.

Beyond that, she taught me some relaxation skills that I still use to this day—breathing exercises, physical activities, and engaging worksheet-based exercises to help me calm myself down and work through what was going on in my busy mind. After just the first few sessions, I felt confident enough to guide myself from then on.

Coupled with other methods for overcoming trauma, CBT has been invaluable; I'll never forget how important it was to my progress. All of this is to say that I highly recommend giving CBT a shot. If it is not for you, then it is not for you; but trying never hurts.

This chapter focused on CBT and some actionable methods that you can employ yourself to work through trauma using a second form of therapy. Now, let's take a look at how diet and nutrition impact PTSD recovery.

Chapter 4:
Diet and Nutrition for PTSD Recovery

Healthy is an outfit that looks different on everybody. —Unknown

Something that I'd wish I'd known sooner was the impact that diet and nutrition can have when it comes to PTSD recovery. If someone had clarified this elusive link to me sooner, I may have jump started my healing process sooner as well! The connection between the mind and the stomach is one that many people overlook, and it is one that I do not want you to miss out on. Truly, understanding how what you do—and do not—eat can impact your recovery process is genuinely life-changing.

My personal journey with nutrition was life-changing. My interest in the healing power of food and its connection to our bodies' well-being started when I struggled with chronic back pain. I noticed stress aggravated the pain, revealing the mind-body connection. After conventional treatments failed, I explored unconventional options, identifying foods causing inflammation through blood tests. Eliminating these foods, along with physical therapy and a Mediterranean-inspired diet, significantly reduced my pain and improved my mood, energy, and sleep. This journey led me to study diet's impact on mental health, specifically focusing on PTSD symptoms.

I want you to be able to experience the same benefits and transformations that I have as a result of diet and nutritional changes. Let's explore the connection together, empowering you with everything you need to know.

Diet, Nutrition, and Mental Health

Believe it or not, the food that you put into your body matters significantly when it comes to healing your mental health. There is a complex yet significant relationship that exists between the brain and the gut, and understanding this relationship is a crucial part of your growth and success when it comes to healing from PTSD.

One way that the brain is impacted by diet includes nutrient intake. Our brain is, in a sense, the center of our body. Every single action that your body carries out, from breathing to thinking and experiencing emotions, starts in the brain. Because the brain is such a busy facilitator when it comes to our lives, it makes sense that the brain would need a wide variety of nutrients in order to function. In specific, the brain thrives on a rich mix of omega-3 fatty acids, vitamins B, C, D, and E, antioxidants, and minerals like zinc and magnesium. When you get enough of all of these components within your diet, your brain is able to function at proper levels.

But why am I telling you all of this science-y stuff? Well, as it turns out, proper nutrition is necessary for the support of neurotransmitters in your brain. In other words, without proper nutrition, your brain cannot send signals from one part of it to the next. This impacts your mental health directly, as neurotransmitters play an essential role in regulating mood and well-being. In essence, unless you have all of the proper nutrients in your body, your brain cannot make sure that you are mentally well off.

In addition, there is something called the gut-brain axis that you should be aware of. The stomach and the brain are connected through this gut-brain axis, which is where the vagus nerve—a nerve running all the way from the brain to the stomach—communicates with chemical messengers like serotonin. When the microbiome in your gut—which you can think of like your gut's environment—is healthy, then your gut-brain axis communication is more likely to be positive. In other words, a flawless, balanced diet allows your stomach to tell your brain that a flawless, balanced mental state is possible! Primarily, this is because a healthy gut minimizes inflammation and aids in the production of neurotransmitters— the chemicals that facilitate brain communication. If your gut biome is not healthy, though, nor will be your mental health.

And it goes without saying that the impact nutrition has on mood is significant. For example, did you know that a nutritional deficiency alone can be enough to cause mood disorders like depression and anxiety? It is true! Simply not eating right can cause a world of problems, including serious mental disorders. In addition to that, diets that are high in processed foods, sugar, and saturated fats—the unhealthiest type of fats— leave someone more susceptible to mental health issues. Eating too much processed food, sugar, etc. can leave you feeling tired, lethargic, sad, and overall be a real downer on your mood, which emphasizes the importance of having a good diet.

Your mood is not the only component of your mental health that is impacted either. Brain function and memory can be impacted as well. For example, balanced nutrition is necessary to various cognitive functions like memory, concentration, and the ability to learn. This means that if you eat a nutritious diet, you are more likely to have strong memory levels, be able to focus better, and be able to retain the things that you learn better. Moreover, antioxidant-rich diets can protect the brain from age-related distress.

Inflammation is tied to your diet as well, which is—you guessed it—also tied to your mental health. In fact, chronic inflammation, something often the result of diet, is linked to the development of various psychiatric disorders. This is because inflammation impacts the brain as well, and the brain cannot really function at optimal levels if it is swollen and inflamed. Anti-inflammatory nutrients can be a life-save in this department, reducing swelling and thus potentially improving your mental health.

Even your blood sugar and energy levels are not left unscathed when it comes to nutrition. Sugar and processed foods can lead to unstable blood sugar levels, which can, in turn, cause mood swings and energy crashes. The best way to employ a diet in order to sustain mood and energy levels is to consume balanced meals that combine proteins with healthy—unsaturated—fats, as well as complex carbohydrates.

Finally, there is a link between stress and nutrition too. Science shows that eating a nutrient-rich diet can help combat the associated negative side effects of stress on mental health. Specifically, magnesium and B-vitamin-rich foods may be best if you are hoping to reduce anxiety and stress.

But how does all of this connect to PTSD? You cannot truly hope to recover from PTSD if you are actively damaging your mental health as a result of your dietary choices. Stress, anxiety, and depression are three of the most common side effects associated with PTSD, and it is clear that eating right can help you overcome these side effects. So while eating a good diet is not going to cure your PTSD, it is going to make the journey a little less strenuous on you.

Essential Nutrients for Well-being

Now that you understand the importance of both bodily and brain health for mental health, it is vital to have sound knowledge of which nutrients are essential to your overall well-being, as well as what foods contain those nutrients. Having foundational knowledge of how food contributes to your holistic well-being will empower you with the information that you need in order to optimize your diet for mental and physical health.

Proteins are the first of several vital nutrients that you need to support your overall health. Proteins serve various functions throughout the body. For example, proteins play a role in repairing muscles and tissues within the body, which is why protein is so necessary for those who exercise especially. But even if you do not work out, you still need protein! Protein is also good for enzymes, which are in charge of digestive functions. Without enzymes, we would not be able to digest the foods that we eat. Hormones are built up by protein too, and particularly notably, neurotransmitters are supported by protein—and we know how important those are. Beyond that, proteins help with the immune system as well as the ability of your hair, skin, and nails to be beautiful. The best sources of protein are meat, poultry, fish, dairy, legumes, nuts, and seeds.

Another important nutrient for your overall well-being is carbohydrates. While diet culture touts carbs as a weight-gain nightmare, they're actually one of three essential macronutrients for the body! They serve as the primary source of energy for the brain and body alike, which means that you absolutely have to have them. Without carbohydrates, you will not be able to store or sustain your energy levels. The best way to get carbohydrates that are healthy for you, however, is going to be in whole grains, vegetables, and fruits—not white bread and other grains like that.

It is also crucial that you get a certain mix of healthy fats in your diet. Saturated and trans fats are the ones to avoid, but the types of fat that we're looking for are monounsaturated fats. These healthy fats are vital for the brain to function as well as for hormone production, and omega-3 fatty acids are necessary for your heart health. You can find monounsaturated fats from sources like olive oil, nuts, and avocados; omega-3 fatty acids can be found in fatty fish, flaxseeds, and chia seeds.

In addition, it is important to get all of the vitamins that your body needs in order to sustain itself. For example, vitamin C is the most important vitamin for your immune system and collagen production. Collagen is the substance that helps our skin maintain elasticity, as well as helps our hair and nails remain strong, which means that vitamin C keeps our hair, skin, and nails thriving while simultaneously boosting our immune system. Citrus fruits are a great source of vitamin C, but you may be surprised to find out that strawberries are an even better source of vitamin C. How delicious! Leafy greens can also provide you with a strong level of vitamin C. As for vitamin D, we need vitamin D for the health of our bones and immune system. The body synthesizes vitamin D from sunlight, fatty fish, and fortified foods. The third most important vitamin(s) are B vitamins, which help with energy production, the functionality of nerves, and our mental well-being over all. B vitamins are most rich in whole grains and leafy greens.

And let's not forget the minerals. Three essential minerals to know about are calcium, magnesium, and iron. Calcium is vital for your bones and muscles, helping them function at optimal levels. Primarily, you can find high levels of calcium in dairy products, leafy greens, and fortified plant milks. Magnesium is good for your muscles and nerves, and it has the added ability to lower stress all on its own. Magnesium is found in nuts, seeds, whole grains, and leafy greens. Then, there's iron—a necessary mineral for the blood to transport oxygen as well as energy production. You can find iron in red meat, beans, fortified cereals, and leafy greens.

Some additional nutrients to keep in mind as well include:

1. Fiber, which is good for digestion and the regulation of blood sugar levels, and found in fruits, vegetables, whole grains, nuts, and seeds.

2. Antioxidants, which protect the body from oxidative stress and reduce the risk of chronic illnesses, are found in brightly colored fruits and vegetables like berries, spinach, and bell peppers.

3. Water, which is vital for hydration.

4. Probiotics, which support a healthy gut and promote digestion and can be found in yogurt, sauerkraut, and kimchi.

You might be wondering why I'm telling you all of this—after all, it may just sound like basic dietary information, and you are here for PTSD information, right? Well, you may be surprised to find that the two connect. As it turns out, if you are deficient in any one of the nutrients that I mentioned above, it can have drastic negative impacts for your mental health. This is because your brain will expend excess energy trying to keep you alive if you do not have enough nutrients, and the first thing to go will be your mental health. In terms of biology, your body will deplete your mental health in an attempt to preserve physical health.

All of this means that you could suffer from nutrient deficiencies, inflammation, and more that make it difficult for your brain to maintain mental health, which in turn can make PTSD recovery near impossible. This is why understanding the perfect balance of nutrients is crucial.

Diets and Supplements

When it comes to PTSD, there are so many recipes and supplements that you can try—ones that are safe and effective for most people. However, throughout my journey with PTSD, I have discovered many different diets, supplements, and other nutritional options that have been instrumental in my success with recovery, and I want to share those with you today!

Nutrition for Stress and Anxiety

I'm sure I do not have to tell you that stress and anxiety can be serious side effects of PTSD as a disorder. If you suffer from PTSD, you also likely deal with stress and/or anxiety every single day. The fortunate news is that a healthy diet can be more beneficial than you realize when it comes to reducing stress and anxiety. For example, some foods and specific nutrients have the ability to lower cortisol levels—the hormone causing stress, as well as to promote relaxation and improve our mental health overall. How incredible! Some dietary ideas that you can incorporate in order to lower your anxiety and stress levels include:

- Consuming complex carbohydrates. As I mentioned earlier, these foods are great for your brain and body. When it comes to anxiety, whole grains can boost serotonin levels, which is a plus—serotonin is responsible for our ability to feel good and at ease.

- Eat plenty of fruits and vegetables. Fruits and vegetables are rich in vitamins, minerals, and antioxidants, all of which play a role in combating stress and inflammation in the body. This can be massively helpful when it comes to mood and stress management.

- Add nuts and seeds to your diet. Nuts and seeds are great sources of healthy fats and essential nutrients. When it comes to nuts and seeds specifically, they provide you with nutrients that your brain and body needs to reduce stress.

- Take advantage of herbal teas. Herbal teas like chamomile are known to have calming properties, thus helping to reduce stress and anxiety while promoting relaxation.

- Eat dark chocolate. Believe it or not, compounds within dark chocolate can promote the release of endorphins, which make us feel good!

- Whole foods are unprocessed, pure foods, including things like fruits, vegetables, whole grains, lean protein, nuts, and seeds. These are all foods that boost your nutrient levels, providing you with the essential nutrients that your mind and body need in order to function. By focusing your diet on whole foods, you get the most out of what you eat, supporting your mind and body in the process.

- Omega-3 fatty acids are able to improve our mood and brain health; they are substances that our body needs to support its natural functions, so it makes sense that a healthy level of omega-3s would be good for us. You can find omega-3s in fatty fish, flaxseeds, and chia seeds primarily, and it is good to note that omega-3s have been linked time and time again to the improvement of certain mental disorders.

- Diet culture will die on the hill that carbs are bad for you, but with a little research you can come to learn that that's not the case at all. Rather, complex carbohydrates serve as the main way for our body to get energy—without them, we feel sluggish, experience blood sugar instability, and more. Therefore, incorporating strong levels of complex carbs into your diet—including brown rice, quinoa, oats, etc.—can keep your blood sugar levels stable as well as contribute to a more balanced mood.

- Probiotics are found in fermented food like yogurt and sauerkraut, and are able to support gut health. Now, there is strong scientific evidence supporting the fact that gut health is fundamentally linked to mental health, which means that incorporating probiotics into your diet can do wonders to improve your mental health!

- Caffeine and alcohol consumption have been notoriously linked with anxiety, mood disruptions, and difficulty sleeping. If you do consume caffeine or alcohol, it is best to do so while you are in a good mindset and while exercising moderation.

- A lot of people tend to avoid drinking water, underestimating the true power it holds when it comes to our health. However, dehydration can play a big role when it comes to negative mood and cognitive function, which means that you should drink enough water throughout the day.

They might seem like small changes, but when it comes down to it, they can make a major impact.

The Mediterranean Diet

Renowned for its health benefits, this diet began in countries surrounding the Mediterranean sea, like Greece, for instance. Some people have observed improvements to stress and anxiety when it comes to engaging in the Mediterranean diet, which is why you might be interested in some of the following benefits:

- This diet is rich in healthy fats, which means that you consume enough omega-3s, which are known to be beneficial for mood and anxiety reduction.

- The diet includes lots of antioxidants, which means that you will get enough fruits, vegetables, whole grains, and other whole foods that contribute to the reduction of anxiety and the overall support of mental health.

- This diet is low in processed foods, which means that you will not be exposed to the negative mood and health impacts that often accompany these foods.

- This diet encourages a balanced nutrient intake, which is beneficial for gut health and mental health overall.

Overall, the Mediterranean diet can offer significant benefits when it comes to reducing stress and anxiety. It is important to understand that no diet is going to cure your PTSD, however. Instead, it is important to mix up approaches for a more holistic benefit.

Herbal Options

I've also had a lot of positive experiences with herbal options—ones that I would love to share with you. Back when I began experiencing chronic back pain, I realized the power of diet and exercise on my physical and mental well-being. I wanted to reduce my reliance on meds, so I started by quitting pain meds successfully. When discussing anti-anxiety meds with my doctor, she unexpectedly increased the dosage. Feeling upset, I took matters into my own hands and gradually tapered off the meds with my general practitioner's support.

Building trust with my doctor allowed me to explore herbal therapy for anxiety. I tried anti-stress and night-time teas and found relief, especially when a constipation tea worked wonders! This sparked my interest in herbs, which I now use in various forms like tea, capsules, and tinctures.

Though herbal remedies are not usually covered by insurance, I enjoy growing and drying herbs myself to save money. Making herbal teas is my go-to DIY method, and I've found honey and tea to be a great combination. It has been a personal journey of discovery and improvement, and I'm glad I explored this path!

In addition, some studies have shown that herbal supplements can prove beneficial when it comes to the reduction of certain PTSD symptoms—specifically when it comes to stress, anxiety, and more. If you prefer to go an herbal route with your treatment, here are some options that are available to you:

- Ashwagandha (Withania somnifera): Ashwagandha, an adaptogenic herb utilized in Ayurvedic medicine, aids in stress adaptation and may potentially alleviate stress and anxiety.

- Chamomile (Matricaria chamomilla): Chamomile's mild sedative and calming effects are often enjoyed as a tea, and a chamomile tincture could offer similar relaxation benefits.

- Lavender (Lavandula angustifolia): Known for its soothing aroma and calming properties, Lavender is frequently used in aromatherapy and can be consumed as a tincture to promote relaxation and reduce anxiety.

- Lion's Mane (Hericium erinaceus): Lion's Mane is an edible mushroom known for its potential neuroprotective and nootropic properties. It contains compounds that stimulate nerve growth factor (NGF) production, which may benefit brain health and cognitive function. Its antioxidant and anti-inflammatory properties further contribute to its neuroprotective effects.

- Passionflower (Passiflora incarnata): With a long history of use for anxiety and insomnia, Passionflower is believed to have sedative effects that aid in promoting relaxation.

- Rhodiola (Rhodiola rosea): As another adaptogenic herb, Rhodiola assists the body in coping with stress and may help alleviate symptoms of anxiety.

- Skullcap (Scutellaria lateriflora): Skullcap's nervine properties are well-known, making it beneficial for calming the nervous system and easing anxiety.

- Valerian (Valeriana officinalis): Valerian, a herb known for its calming properties, may be particularly useful for individuals experiencing sleep disturbances due to PTSD.

The best thing that you can do with these herbs is to make a tea out of them, but if you are looking for something different, you can always make a tincture!

How to Make a Tincture

Making a tincture is rather simple! You will need the following ingredients:

- Amber glass dropper bottles for storage

- Clean glass jar with a tight-fitting lid

- Dried or fresh herbs of your choice (e.g., lavender, chamomile, valerian, etc.)

- High-proof alcohol (such as vodka, brandy, or grain alcohol) with at least 40% alcohol content (80 proof or higher)

- Cheesecloth or fine mesh strainer

Also, keep in mind that if you are averse to using alcohol, you can substitute apple cider vinegar!

In order to make your tincture, follow these steps:

1. If you are using fresh herbs, finely chop or grind them to unleash their active constituents. For dried herbs, gently crush them to increase their surface area for extraction.

2. Grab a clean glass jar and put the prepared herbs inside, filling it about one-third to one-half full. Choose a jar size that matches the amount of tincture you want to make.

3. Pour your high-proof alcohol over the herbs until they are completely covered, leaving some space at the top. Ensure the alcohol fully covers the plant material.

4. Remember to label the jar with the herb's name and the date you made it. This helps keep track of the tincture's strength and expiration date.

5. Seal the jar tightly and place it in a cool, dark spot like a cupboard. Let the herbs steep in the alcohol for about 4 to 6 weeks. Give the jar a gentle shake every day or so to help with extraction.

6. After the extraction period, strain the tincture using a cheesecloth or fine mesh strainer into a clean bowl. Squeeze the herbs to get as much liquid as possible.

7. Transfer the strained tincture into amber glass dropper bottles to preserve its potency. Store the bottles in a cool, dark place.

The dosage you need is going to depend on various circumstances, which is why it is good to always contact an herbalist before engaging with a tincture; however, generally a few drops does the trick. There are also a few safety precautions to keep in mind when it comes to tinctures. First, you are going to want to research the herb and ensure that it is safe. Keep in mind that certain herbs are not suitable for those with underlying health conditions, or those who are pregnant or nursing. Pay attention to any medications you are on as well, because some interact negatively with herbs. Finally, do not use rubbing alcohol or denatured alcohol for your tinctures—doing so can be life threatening.

Exercise and Lifestyle Changes for PTSD

The last thing that I want to talk to you about when it comes to diet and nutrition is exercise. Exercise is so important for your body, but what I really want to tell you about is how exercise can improve your mental health, as well as how to begin your exercise regime, exercising on a busy schedule, and much more.

I used to despise exercising! But with my little one's enthusiasm for playgrounds, pool, and bike rides during this time of year, I naturally end up moving more. What really kicked off my exercise routine, though, was physical therapy. Having appointments three times a week made it a consistent part of my life, and soon enough, I developed a habit and felt "off" when I skipped a day. Surprisingly, I began looking forward to my workouts! Even now, what keeps me motivated is accountability. Whether it is my daughter encouraging me or a coworker suggesting a walk break, or the gym staff calling me out if I'm absent for a few days, having someone to keep me on track is what works for me!

Benefits of Exercise for Mental Health

When it comes to exercise, much like the foods that you do and do not eat, there are numerous benefits that apply when it comes to mental health. Exercise has the ability to promote mental and emotional well-being, as well as the reduction of mental health disorders.

One way that this occurs is through the enhancement of mood. Exercise is a well-known mood booster! Throughout the process of exercising, the physical activity that you engage in notably stimulates the release of endorphins. Endorphins are the body's natural means of elevating mood, which can cause you to feel relaxed or even happy as a result of exercising. Moreover, exercise is known to help alleviate some of the symptoms of depression and anxiety, therefore naturally improving your emotional well-being—no strings attached!

Stress reduction is another benefit that accompanies regular physical activity. As it turns out, regular exercise can lower cortisol levels, which is the hormone that causes stress. In turn, this leads to the reduction of feelings like stress, tension, and anxiety. What's more is that exercising can serve as a healthy way to release pent up stress and frustration. Many PTSD survivors find solace in exercise, using it as a means to build strength and courage alike. In more ways than one, exercising regularly serves to be a valuable component of mental health and healing.

And that's not even all of the benefits. But now, you may be wondering how you can take advantage of all of these awesome benefits for your health when it comes to exercise. It is simple—all you have to do is get started!

How to Start Working Out

Getting started with exercise is easy! One of the first things I can recommend is to contact your primary care provider before beginning a new exercise program, which is essential if you have existing health concerns. This is because things like heart conditions, blood pressure issues, and more can all be impacted by your exercise habits, and no one wants to end up inadvertently damaging their health! Because of this, reach out to your doctor if you can.

The next thing that you need to do is set clear goals for your exercise routines. Setting goals is a good next step because goals empower you in many ways. For one, they allow you to know exactly what you want to accomplish. This knowledge equips you to handle both achievements and setbacks, which is an excellent way to stay motivated. Moreover, all good goals are time-bound. What this means is that your goal will have a time limit on it, wherein after a certain amount of time, you should have achieved a certain milestone. Time-based goals may feel like a lot of pressure at first, but over time, you will come to realize that they're good for you; a strong, time-sensitive goal prevents you from constantly moving the markers for success back and forth, thus helping you to achieve more. Your goals for exercise can be anything you want, from fitness to weight changes and stress reduction, all the way to improving your well-being.

The next piece of advice that I have for you is to start small, and pick activities that you actually enjoy engaging with. Starting your exercise habit off with something far too intense is only going to burn you out and leave you feeling uninspired to continue. Therefore, it is important to set small and realistic goals. Plus, you should pick activities that you actually enjoy; otherwise, you are not actually going to exercise if it is not something that you look forward to. Make sure that you also schedule in warm-up and cool down time as well, and try to stick to a schedule that follows a daily or weekly rotation.

It might be better for some people to keep accountable through the employment of technology and a workout partner. Using fitness apps, activity trackers, and other forms of tech can truly up your ability to keep working out, and that's extra helpful when it comes to getting a workout buddy. Workout buddies can motivate you with some friendly competition or general accountability check ups, depending on your preference.

You should also take stock of your progress, be patient, and reward yourself. Remember to stay hydrated and you will do great!

Exercise on a Busy Schedule

I'll be the first to admit that working out on a busy schedule can be... hard. When it seems like you are already low on time, of course you are not going to be chomping at the bit to find additional time to do something like exercising. Fortunately, with these helpful tips, you can successfully squeeze in some exercise with ease—even for the most busy of schedules!

- Engage in short, high-intensity workouts that can be completed in 15-20 minutes, yet pack a big punch.

- If you do not have time to complete a full workout all at once, consider breaking it into segments instead. For example, do three 10-minute sessions instead of one 30-minute session.

- Walk or bike to work if you can, or even consider walking part of the way to work to maximize your commute.

- Go on a quick walk during your lunch break.

- Buy equipment such as bicycle chairs and other equipment that you can use while working at home or even just relaxing.

- Take the stairs instead of the elevator.

- Wake up a bit early to get some extra exercise in.

- Above all, be consistent.

Now, you understand all of the key aspects of diet and wellness that are going to support your PTSD recovery, including some snazzy recipes and supplements to help you along the way. Let's move on to explore the power of prayers for peace!

Chapter 5:
The Power of Prayers for Peace

Healing takes courage, and we all have courage, even if we have to dig a little to find it. —Tori Amos

I am a Christian and firmly believe in the healing powers of God. If you're not religious or don't want to hear about my experience with Christianity, please skip to the meditation section of this chapter.

One of the best decisions of my life was finding God. God and the power of prayer were instrumental to my healing process. He pulled me out of some of the darkest times in my life, and now I want to share that connection I've found with you. Now, this is not me trying to convert you to my religion— far from it. If you are already religious, seeking religion, religiously curious, or even spiritually inclined, there's something for you in this chapter. I'm sharing my journey with you so that you can find something meaningful from it, or perhaps even find your own path after hearing about mine. So, without any further delay, let's talk about how prayer and faith in God can help you overcome struggles pertaining to your PTSD.

Spirituality and Religion in Healing

Many people recognize the fact that religion and spirituality alike have an astounding ability to help us heal and recover, especially when it comes to PTSD. Strong faith is associated with stronger healing results, which, in my opinion, is a quite beautiful aspect of religion. Some of the many ways that religion can help us overcome struggles we face include:

- Providing us with meaning and purpose. Both religion and spirituality alike have a striking ability to provide us with a sense of meaning and purpose in life. Personally, after experiencing forms of trauma, I know it was hard for me to grapple with a sense of purpose. That's something that religion helped me with; it helped me embody purpose and find direction in life.

- Connecting us with others. Most religions and spiritualities have the ability to connect us with community and social support. Especially if your religion is organized, meaning that it has church—or similar—meetings, then you can meet people with your same beliefs and offer each other emotional, practical, and social

- Introduction to coping mechanisms. Intrinsically, religion and spirituality provide us with coping mechanisms for hardship. Through concepts like prayers, meditation, mindfulness, and rituals, we can come to a place where it is easier to manage our emotions and stressors, remain calm, and even develop hope, which leads me to my next point.

- Providing hope and optimism. Believing in a higher power or higher force does wonders for impacting our mindset and attitude in a positive way. Religious people like me believe that God is here to take care of us, and that belief is beautiful and so uplifting!

- Promoting positive lifestyle choices. Most religions make it a point to promote beneficial lifestyle choices to help us boost our physical healing and overall well-being through avoiding substance use, poor dietary choices, and a lack of self-care.

And that's just the start of the benefits that religion and spirituality can offer us when it comes to healing from PTSD and other issues in life. Through the power of religion and spirituality, we can truly unlock the path for us to heal.

PTSD can be an all-consuming force. In my hardest times, it's rewarding to keep in mind that in Psalms, it implies that we can turn to the Lord in our times of misery and need and wait for Him to come to our aid. This can be a powerful reminder for the times where you feel alone and abandoned.

Prayer Techniques for Peace and Inner Strength

Did you know that there are many different methods for prayer, each of which offering different benefits when it comes to the healing process? There are, and I do not just mean the way you stand or sit when you pray! No, there are actually three techniques that I want to tell you about today so that you can find the methods of prayer that work best for you and your healing. The three methods I want to tell you about include intercessory prayer, supplicatory prayer, and mindfulness meditation prayer.

Intercessory prayer is a type of prayer where we pray on behalf of others. What does this have to do with your PTSD healing? Well, a lot of intercessory prayer occurs when groups or individuals pray for the health or healing of others. Your family, church, or friends can pray on behalf of your healing if you hope to use intercessory prayer for your own recovery. It is also possible that praying for others can help you recover too. Praying for other people is a divine act of kindness wherein we take the time to extend our love and hope to other people. This can help us heal by making us feel better and helping us connect to other people. Moreover, intercessory prayer has psychological benefits when it comes to support and stress reduction, and it provides us with an uncanny sense of hope. Even if you personally do not believe in God, research indicates that prayer can be good for our hope and minds even still.

Next is supplicatory prayer. Supplicatory prayer involves praying for ourselves, sort of like intercessory prayer, in request of something specific from a higher power. You can specifically request that God help you heal from your trauma and PTSD among other things, and supplicatory prayer can be immensely beneficial when it comes to the healing process. Supplicatory prayer helps us express our needs and desires to God or another deity, which can help you put your pain and struggles into words. Prayer is also a fabulous coping mechanism, allowing someone kind and trustworthy to hear what we're going through.

Mindfulness meditation prayer is another form of prayer combining mindful awareness of your presence with prayer, usually supplicatory prayer. By being mindful, you are more able to receive messages from higher powers, as well as connect with yourself and your deity at the same time.

A final prayer technique that I want to share with you is a common prayer layout that you can use. While memorizing prayers—as you may do with the ones below—is a wonderful way to connect with God, making your own, unique prayers up through something like this is amazing too:

1. Praise God. Start your prayer with kind words that praise God for all He does for you and the world around you.

2. Pray for work in the world. Pray for improvements that can be made to the world around you before moving on to more "selfish" personal prayers.

3. Pray for your daily needs. This includes things like shelter and basic resources—it's always a good idea to pray to *keep* these things in your life.

4. Pray for forgiveness. We all sin; this is one of your opportunities to request forgiveness.

5. Pray for help with daily struggles. Lastly, you're going to pray for help with specific struggles; this is where praying for PTSD healing comes in.

Feel free to modify the above framework as needed!

Finally, it's important to remember that forgiveness is a challenging task and you may need to ask God for help with this. From personal experience, I know that when you turn your judgment and your anger, all of the frustration and hatred you feel, over to God for judgment, you truly begin to forgive in a stronger sense than you ever have before.

Specific Prayers to Implement Into Your Life

When it comes to prayer, it's good to remember that there's no right or wrong way to pray, as long as it comes from the heart. A formal, memorized prayer can be just as meaningful as a casual conversation with God, so long as you have that intention in your heart. Please keep this in mind as you read through this section.

Through my years of religion and forming a personal relationship with God, I've developed a backlog of prayers that I love to use in times of need. I want to share those prayers with you now:

- "Come to me, all you who are weary and burdened, and I will give you rest. Take my yoke upon you and learn from me, for I am gentle and humble in heart, and you will find rest for your souls." —Matthew 11:28-29

- "Lord, it is so easy to fall into worry. When my fears are reverberating in my mind, help me stop trying to fix everything myself. Teach me to turn to You in prayer, trust You to be in charge and let Your peace reign over me. In Jesus' Name, Amen." — Francine Rivers

- "You know that we live in a crazy and chaotic world. You also know my struggles in my daily life. When life gets to be too much, please help me come to you. Calm my thoughts and emotions and open my heart to your peace, comfort, and wisdom. Help me not to live in fear. Please reduce the feelings of fear and anxiety that plague me. Help me rest in You and trust You as I navigate through this broken world. In Your name I pray, Jesus. Amen." —Carrie Lorance

- "Lord, you know me. You made me. You love me. Meet me where I am in this moment. You knew I'd be here. Do what You want with my churning insides and my spinning mind and my blown-up fear. Do not waste a minute of my anxiety. Heal it. Use it. Change it.

44

Instead of begging for something specific, I give myself to You. What do you want from me and for me? Thank you for understanding me when no one else does and loving me anyway. In Jesus' Name, Amen." —Lori Freeland

- "Heavenly Father, thank You for being an overcoming God! I know I can take heart because You have overcome the world. Empower me to rise above my circumstances. Help me cast my anxiety on You because You care for me. Give me Your power to overcome. Thank You for giving me the victory! In Jesus' Name, Amen." — Esther Fleece Allen

- "Dear Father, In this space of total anxiety, I'm praying to you, the God of all. Jesus, I need you so much. The weight of this world consumes my heart and my spirit is confused. I know you are not the god of confusion; you are the God of order, love and peace. I pray you would restore order right now in me. May my mind perceive that you make me sound. May my soul receive that you give me strength. May my heart believe that you show me love. Thank you for the relief of an unburdened heart. Amen." —Rachel Wojo

- "Father, my heart is heavy. I feel like I have to carry the burden alone. Words like overwhelmed, distraught, exhausted seem to describe where I am. I am not sure how to let you carry my heavy load, so please show me how. Take it from me. Let me rest and be refreshed so that my heart will not be so heavy in the morning. In Jesus' name. Amen." —Ron Moore

- "Father, You know that sometimes life and the circumstances we face are just hard. But you are our source of peace. I pray for the one reading these words right now. I pray that whatever they are facing right now, that they would take a deep breath and inhale more of you and your peace while exhaling any of the worries that weigh them down. I pray that they would be anxious for nothing, but would come to you in prayer with all their needs, thanking you even now that you know how you are going to take care of every last detail. I thank you that you care about the things that we care about, and that you are our source of peace in the midst of the storms. In Jesus' name, Amen." —Dr. Michelle Bengston

- "I know that worrying gets me nowhere. Yet I still allow worry and anxiety to consume me. In times such as these, Lord, I ask you to grant me a great amount of strength, faith, and courage to fight off the doubt and fear within my minds. Faith casts out fear while fear casts out faith." —Unknown

- "Loving God, Please grant me peace of mind and calm my troubled heart. My soul is like a turbulent sea. I cannot seem to find my balance so I stumble and worry constantly. Give me the strength and clarity of mind to find my purpose and walk the path you have laid out for me. I trust your Love God, and know that you will heal this stress. Just as the sun rises each day against the dark of night. Please bring me clarity with the light of God. In your name I pray, Amen." —Unknown

- Heavenly Father, When I feel crushed by my own worries, life my mind and help me to see the truth. When fear grips me tight and I feel like I cannot move, free my heart and help me to take things one step at a time. When I cannot express the turmoil inside, calm me with your quiet words of love. I choose to trust in You, each day, each hour, each moment of my life. I know deep down that I [am] in Your grace, forgiven, restored by Your sacrifice, You have set me free. Amen." —Unknown

- "Dear God, I come before You to lay my panic and anxiety at Your feet. When I'm crushed by my fears and worries, remind me of Your power and Your grace. Fill me with Your peace as I trust in You and You alone. I know I cannot beat this on my own, but I also know that I have You, Lord, and You have already paid the ultimate price to carry my burdens. For this I thank you, Amen." — Unknown

When you feel in need of some support from the Lord, any of these prayers will do the trick.

Non-religious Spirituality for Healing

But what do you do if you are not religious? Well, there are a number of spiritual practices, some of which may suit your needs. And remember, these practices can absolutely be supported by including the Lord as the focal point of your practice, relying on Him to bring about the benefits rather than putting the healing power in the alternative methods themselves—allowing Christians to benefit from these methods too. Below are some guides for starting with meditation, crystal healing, and positive affirmations for PTSD recovery.

Meditation

Meditation is a powerful tool that anyone can use regardless of faith. Meditation can help your PTSD recovery process in many ways. For example, meditation is known to help resolve stress and anxiety through methods like breathing, mindfulness, and more, which triggers the brain and body to feel relaxed. Meditation can also help regulate certain emotions, especially ones that are overwhelming. Furthermore, when it comes to PTSD, meditation can help us reprocess traumatic memories—almost how EMDR works its magic—in order to revoke some of the negative side effects of trauma. Sleep, neuroplasticity, and positive mindsets can also be improved through meditation.

My favorite method of meditating is to look up videos or audios on YouTube, Headspace, or other platforms. Depending on your goals for your meditation, there are a few different types of meditation to take advantage of:

- Mindfulness Meditation: Mindfulness meditation involves paying non-judgmental attention to the present moment, including your thoughts, feelings, bodily sensations, and the surrounding environment. It aims to cultivate awareness, acceptance, and a deep understanding of your experiences.

- Transcendental Meditation (TM): TM is a mantra-based meditation technique where practitioners silently repeat a specific mantra to help quiet the mind and access a state of deep relaxation and inner stillness.

- Loving-Kindness Meditation (Metta): This practice involves generating feelings of compassion, love, and kindness toward oneself and others. It often includes repeating specific phrases or affirmations to cultivate positive emotions and connections.

- Guided Meditation: In guided meditation, a recorded voice or a meditation guide leads you through a meditation session. This can be helpful for beginners, as the guide provides instructions and imagery to help you relax and focus.

- Body Scan Meditation: This involves systematically directing your attention to different parts of the body, observing sensations, and releasing tension. It is a way to promote relaxation, mindfulness, and body awareness.

- Breath Awareness Meditation: Breath awareness meditation centers on observing your breath as it naturally flows in and out. Focusing on the breath can help anchor your attention and promote relaxation.

- Zen Meditation (Zazen): Zazen is a form of seated meditation practiced in Zen Buddhism. It involves sitting in a specific posture and focusing on the breath, letting thoughts come and go without attachment.

- Vipassana Meditation: Also known as insight meditation, Vipassana encourages the observation of thoughts, sensations, and emotions in a detached and non-reactive manner to gain insight into the nature of reality.

- Chakra Meditation: Derived from Hindu and yogic traditions, chakra meditation focuses on the body's energy centers (chakras) to balance and harmonize the flow of energy throughout the body.

- Walking Meditation: This practice involves walking slowly and mindfully, paying attention to each step, your breath, and your surroundings. It is often practiced outdoors to connect with nature.

- Body Movement Meditation: Practices like Tai Chi, Qigong, and Yoga can be considered forms of movement meditation. These combine physical movement with breath awareness and mindfulness.

- Sound Meditation: Using sound as a focal point, practitioners might listen to soothing music, chanting, or sounds from nature to induce a meditative state.

- Mantra Meditation: Similar to TM, mantra meditation involves repeating a specific word, phrase, or sound (mantra) to help focus the mind and achieve a state of relaxation.

- Visualization Meditation: Visualization involves creating mental images of peaceful or positive scenes. It can be used to reduce stress, enhance focus, and promote relaxation.

The thing to remember about meditation is that the best results come from routine. Most people who meditate say that it takes about three weeks for results to show up, but when they do, those results are astounding. Religious or not, I recommend trying meditation for yourself.

Positive Affirmations

Positive affirmations can be written down, spoken aloud to yourself, or even thought in your head to reprogram negative thought processes. Some positive affirmations for PTSD include:

- I am resilient, and I am healing at my own pace.

- I deserve peace, and I am working towards finding it within myself.

- I am not defined by my past. I am creating a brighter future for myself.

- I am strong enough to face my challenges and embrace my growth.

- I am safe in this present moment, and I choose to let go of what no longer serves me.

- I am worthy of love, care, and healing, and I extend this to myself each day.

- I have the power to reframe my thoughts and transform my perspective.

- I am in control of my reactions, and I choose peace over fear.

- I am releasing the weight of trauma and embracing a lighter, more hopeful outlook on life.

- I am on a journey of healing, and each step I take brings me closer to wholeness and well-being.

Religion can be a powerful catalyst for the process of our recovery. Even if you do not find the same connection with religion that I have, spiritual practices that are non-religious can help you as well. Even if you do not want to include religion or spirituality into your healing process—which is entirely valid—there are still plenty of healing options for you, which we're going to delve into more right now.

Chapter 6:
Identifying Triggers and Building Resilience

It is your reaction to adversity, not adversity itself that determines how your life's story will develop. —Dieter F. Uchtdorf

Everyone knows about the phrase "trigger warning" due to a popular social media tendency from a few years ago to mock those with triggers. Triggers became such a big joke that a lot of people do not know that triggers are a very real, serious thing—often a symptom that results from trauma and mental illness. It is very important to me that you understand that triggers are a valid aspect of mental health and trauma. Misunderstanding what a trigger is and how it can impact one's life is a very isolating experience. I remember spending years wondering if my triggers were invalid due to the mockery triggers as a concept faces. Now, though, I know that triggers are valid, and by identifying your triggers, you can build resilience and manage those triggers for a life that is not controlled by them.

Understanding Triggers and Their Impact on PTSD

Even if you do not think you have triggers, if you have PTSD, you probably have triggers. Are there ever certain experiences, events, statements, or other concepts that make you feel... trapped? They might make you feel as though you felt in the moment of your trauma—scared, abandoned, or even angry. When something makes you feel so uncontrollably emotive, it is likely a trigger.

What is a trigger in terms of psychology, though? From a psychological standpoint, a trigger is defined as a form of sensory input that can cause painful memories or certain symptoms to resurface (Pedersen, 2022). You might remember certain sights, sounds, smells, or feelings that accompanied. your trauma, and when you re-encounter that stimuli, it can make you feel just like you did in the moment. Typically, triggers form due to a mental connection that links stimuli to memories. Even if a scent, for example, does not consciously remind you of your trauma, your mind can make that connection anyway. Some examples of common triggers that people experience include:

- Loud noises
- Strong odors
- Stress
- Traumatic memories
- Crowded spaces
- Social situations
- Certain foods
- Change in routine
- Criticism
- Abandonment
- Rejection
- Failure
- Public speaking
- Financial problems
- Health issues
- Relationship conflicts
- Loss of a loved one
- Uncertainty

Even if you do not recognize your trigger on that list, it can still be considered a valid trigger. In correlation to PTSD, a trigger can, well, trigger the symptoms of that disorder. For example, if you were in a traumatic car accident, being on the road again can be a trigger. COVID-19 serves as a trigger for many to this day, with masks, coughing, and isolation proving to activate one's fight or flight. In my case, certain things trigger my PTSD too. And when PTSD is triggered, it can lead to a few different things.

One thing that can happen when PTSD is triggered is an internal impact.

Some people shut down when triggered, going into a mental state, panic attack, or being unable to act as a result of their trigger. For others, that reaction is more external. If you have ever seen a veteran or someone with gun-related trauma react harshly to fireworks, then you have a small window into what an external trigger may look like.

Generally, understanding your triggers is important because it allows you to understand a few things. Understanding your triggers can:

- Help you know what to avoid and what to work on if you are hoping to overcome your triggers.

- Allow you to anticipate reactions as a result of triggers.

- Help you build up resilience and appropriate coping mechanisms.

And much more. Finding an in-depth understanding of your triggers is the best way to get to know yourself and your trauma in a way that allows you to heal and recover. When you do not understand your triggers, you cannot truly begin the process of recovery in the truest way possible. Let's take a look at what exactly you can do for identifying and managing your triggers.

Strategies for Identifying and Managing Triggers

With your newfound knowledge of how a trigger can impact you and why it is important to learn about your triggers, you are probably wondering what you can do to even identify your triggers in the first place. After all, it is not always obvious what your triggers are, especially not until you are actually triggered. And by the time you have been triggered, it is too late; you are in for an experience you likely do not want to have, possibly in front of other people. While you cannot always predict or identify your triggers ahead of time, there are some things that you can do in order to make the process of identifying those triggers easier.

12 Steps to Identifying Triggers

During my time and experience with what it is like to have PTSD, I've developed a bit of a process that can help you out too. Here is a 12-step process for identifying your triggers:

1. Self-awareness. The first step in the process of identifying your

triggers is to develop a heightened sense of self-awareness. This can be developed by focusing on both your emotional and physical reactions in various situations, as well as the thoughts that you have around certain circumstances. By keeping track of how you feel and respond at various times, you enable yourself to understand your own mind; you develop the ability to understand why certain things provoke certain responses.

2. Keep a journal. It might sound like a lot of work, or as though it is not worth it, but keeping a journal to record what you feel, your experiences, and the reactions you perpetuate throughout the day is a good way to pay attention to how certain things make you feel. Note down any moments when you feel heightened stress, anxiety, anger, or other strong emotions. This can be indicative of circumstances that lead up to triggers or more minor triggers themselves.

3. Reflect on patterns. Once you have spent some time working on your journal, maybe a few days or even a few weeks, it can be a good idea to go back over those entries that you have made in order to reflect on patterns that trace through your emotional responses. Are there specific situations or circumstances that consistently lead to certain emotional reactions? If so, you may be on the verge of identifying a trigger.

4. Analyze your intense emotions. With and without your journal, take the time to identify when your emotions are particularly intense. When you do feel those intense emotions, ask yourself what you were experiencing just before you began to feel that way. Try to pinpoint the trigger that might have set off those emotions, and you will be able to understand which events bring out strong emotions in you.

5. Consider physical responses. A lot of people overlook just how telling physical responses can be when it comes to pinpointing triggers. Pay special attention to the physical sensations that you feel in certain situations. Some signs that you might want to look out for include an increased heart rate, shallow breathing, and muscle tension. Other physical symptoms can indicate a trigger as well.

6. Examine your past experiences. Make sure that you are in a strong mindset for it, as you will probably bring up some painful emotions when you do think about these past experiences. By making sure that you are in a good mindset, you do not have to worry about it being the "right" time. Consider especially traumatic or emotional experiences and see if you can link those experiences to a past

event; this can tell you where a strong emotional impact is found.

7. Seek professional help. If you are struggling to identify your triggers on your own, it might be a good idea to consult with a counselor or therapist about it. I know not everyone has access to something like this, which is why you can feel free to skip this step and go to the next one if you do not have the means.

8. Use guided visualization. Guided visualization is a strong method for helping you place yourself in different scenarios without feeling that way. Imagine yourself in different scenarios—even if they did not happen to you—to see what your emotional and physical reactions are like. This is a great exercise for helping you reveal triggers that are not immediately obvious.

9. Discuss the situation with trusted individuals. Talk to close friends, family members, or confidants about your emotional responses. Sometimes, those around you might notice patterns or triggers that you are not fully aware of.

10. Experiment with exposure. Gradually expose yourself to situations that you suspect might be triggers. Monitor your reactions closely to see if they align with your suspicions.

11. Practice mindfulness. Engage in mindfulness techniques to stay present in the moment. This can help you observe your thoughts and emotions without immediate reaction, making it easier to identify triggers.

12. Have patience. Identifying triggers can be a gradual process. It might take time to connect the dots between your emotions and specific situations. Be patient with yourself throughout this journey.

You do not have to memorize these steps; you can revisit them in this book at any time! Now, we have to focus on what to do with your triggers once you have identified them.

Managing Identified Triggers

Now, you are probably wondering how you can manage your triggers. Luckily for you, I have a list of tips to share:

*   Recognize your triggers. Use the insights you have gained from identifying triggers to become more aware of situations that might

lead to heightened emotional reactions.

- Practice deep breathing exercises when you feel triggered. Focus on slow, deep breaths to help calm your nervous system and reduce the intensity of your emotional response.

- Engage in mindfulness techniques or grounding exercises. Focus on your senses and the present moment to redirect your thoughts away from the trigger.

- Develop a plan for when you encounter triggers. Identify safe spaces or activities that help you feel calm and secure, and use them as a retreat when needed.

- Challenge negative thoughts and self-talk that arise from triggers. Replace them with positive and rational affirmations to help regain control over your emotions.

- Keep yourself occupied with activities that divert your attention away from the trigger. This could be hobbies, reading, exercise, or any other enjoyable and engaging task.

- Practice progressive muscle relaxation to release tension from your body. Tense and then relax different muscle groups, which can help reduce stress and anxiety.

- While working on managing triggers, consider minimizing your exposure to situations or stimuli that consistently lead to strong emotional reactions.

- Reach out to friends, family, or support groups when you are dealing with triggers. Sharing your feelings can provide comfort and validation.

- Explore therapeutic approaches like cognitive behavioral therapy (CBT) or dialectical behavior therapy (DBT), which provide tools to manage and cope with triggers.

- Prioritize your physical well-being by getting enough sleep, maintaining a balanced diet, and engaging in regular exercise. Physical health can influence emotional resilience.

- Learn and practice relaxation techniques such as meditation, yoga, or tai chi to promote relaxation and emotional regulation.

- When you feel a trigger, close your eyes and visualize a calm, peaceful scene. This can help shift your focus away from the trigger and reduce anxiety.

- If triggers significantly impact your daily life, consider working with a mental health professional. They can provide tailored strategies and support.

- Establish boundaries with people and situations that consistently trigger negative emotions. Learn to say no and prioritize your well-being.

- Replace negative coping mechanisms (like substance use) with healthy ones that promote well-being and emotional balance.

With these tips, you are well on your way to managing those triggers. Do not worry if you need more help with one of those tips; the next few sessions should cover it!

Building Resilience Through Coping Mechanisms

Resilience is our ability to bounce back from a situation that bothers us. When someone is a resilient individual, they have the ability to shake something negative off and overcome it, going back to their usual self after the fact. When you have PTSD, however, this might sound like a foreign concept; it can feel really hard to bounce back from anything when everything is so overwhelming. The good news is that everyone has the potential to be resilient, and that includes you. For a PTSD survivor, coping mechanisms are the best way to develop resilience. There are hundreds of coping mechanisms that you can develop to improve your life, but we only have the time to talk about a handful of them—let's jump on it!

Positive Reframing

When you survive something bad—or even when you have just had negative thoughts—it can be really easy to get trapped in a cycle of negativity. That negativity can turn a good situation bad and a bad situation worse. Positive reframing has the power to help you look at a situation from all angles. Positive reframing does not mean being a blind optimist; it means finding the silver lining or opportunities for growth that can arise from a difficult circumstance, and knowing that this, too, shall pass even if it feels like the end of the world. By working to reframe your negative thoughts into positive or even neutral ones, you take the power away from those negative thoughts and pave the road for your own future.

Emotional Awareness

Emotional awareness is another tactic that will allow you to have the power to take control over your life. Emotional awareness is exactly what it sounds like; it involves knowing not only what you feel in the moment, but why you feel it. Learning to recognize and label your emotions for what they are will help you choose other appropriate coping strategies that coincide with this one, helping you to find the best motion forward.

Problem-Solving Skills

The next coping mechanism you should master for resilience includes problem-solving. For someone with PTSD, it can feel like there are so many problems around and we cannot solve any of them. However, if you master problem-solving skills, you gain the ability to find practical solutions to challenges rather than dwelling on the problem itself. One way that you can work on problem-solving skills is to break down issues into manageable steps, and then take action toward solving that problem.

Healthy Relationships

Forming healthy relationships with those around you is another coping mechanism that you can take advantage of. I know that my relationship with those in my life, especially my beautiful daughter, have gotten me through some tough times. By forging healthy relationships, you have someone to rely on in tough times—someone to talk to for advice as well as someone willing to show you that you are worthy of care. Cultivating a support network of friends, family, and mentors is a phenomenal way to share your feelings with trusted individuals who can provide comfort and support. Even if it does not feel like you know anyone in real life who can support you, coworkers and event support groups online can provide you with essential support.

Mindfulness Meditation

A lot of people look past mindfulness meditation as a good solution and coping mechanism, but they should not! Engaging with mindfulness meditation can be amazingly beneficial when it comes to being resilient about both your past trauma and the future situations you will encounter. Engage in mindfulness practices to stay present and reduce rumination about past or future stressors; this can enhance your emotional resilience. I highly recommend using videos online to guide you through mindfulness meditation, especially at first. That will make it easier to get into the swing of things.

Physical Well-being

It surprised me when I found out, but physical health can serve as a great coping mechanism and actually plays a wonderful role in PTSD recovery. When you feel immense stress, sadness, or anger, physically moving around to get it all out of you is a good way to go. Exercise like running, machine workouts, or even easy yoga stretches can raise your endorphins and make you feel better when you are down. It is also really good for emotional regulation as well. Making sure to eat enough food and get enough sleep can make your brain feel better and regulate your mood too, which is another good reason to watch out for your physical well-being. After all, a healthy body supports a resilient mind!

Stress-Relief Activities

Something else you can do for a coping mechanism is to engage with activities that you enjoy and relieve your stress. This is highly subjective, as what makes you feel less stressed is different than what will make me feel less stressed. Whether it is reading, art, music, or sports, these activities provide an outlet for stress and boost mood. For me, stress relief is as simple as connecting with nature—tuning into the lovely sounds of the birds and feeling the sun shine down on me. But for others, that might not be enough—which is totally alright.

Cognitive Restructuring

Cognitive restructuring is a common coping mechanism that a lot of therapists teach their clients. This is similar to positive reframing, as it involves challenging negative thought patterns to replace them with more balanced or realistic ones. This can prevent you from spiraling into anxiety or depression.

Journaling

I find a lot of value in writing down my thoughts. It reminds me that things always seem worse inside of my mind than they truly are in real life. By writing down my thoughts, I can get some distance from them, which really helps; I recommend you do the same.

All of these coping mechanisms and more can help you uncover what you are feeling and channel those triggers into more productive outlets, stopping them before they can harm you or dealing with the aftermath more peacefully.

Self-Care Practices for Stress Management and Anxiety Reduction

Taking care of yourself is a really underrated way of caring for yourself. When it comes to self-care for reducing stress and anxiety, here is a list of tips that I've learned and want to share with you today:

- Engage in mindfulness meditation to stay present and reduce anxiety. Focus on your breath and observe your thoughts without judgment.

- Practice deep breathing techniques, like diaphragmatic breathing or the 4-7-8 technique, to calm your nervous system and reduce stress.

- Tense and then relax different muscle groups in your body to release physical tension and promote relaxation.

- Engage in regular physical activity to release endorphins, which are natural mood enhancers. Exercise can also reduce stress hormones.

- Consume a balanced diet rich in whole foods, fruits, vegetables, lean proteins, and healthy fats. Avoid excessive caffeine and sugar.

- Prioritize getting enough quality sleep. Create a calming bedtime routine and maintain a consistent sleep schedule.

- Set boundaries for screen time and digital devices, especially before bedtime. Technology can contribute to stress and disrupt sleep.

- Spend time outdoors and connect with nature. A walk in a park or a hike can be refreshing and calming.

- Write down your thoughts, emotions, and experiences. Journaling can help you process your feelings and gain clarity.

- Engage in creative activities like drawing, painting, crafting, or playing a musical instrument. Expressing yourself creatively can be

60

therapeutic.

- Take relaxing baths or showers to soothe your muscles and unwind. Consider using calming essential oils or bath salts.

- Eat slowly and savor your meals. Pay attention to the taste, texture, and smell of your food.

- Repeat positive affirmations to counter negative self-talk and boost self-esteem.

- Spend quality time with family and friends who uplift and support you. Social connections are essential for well-being.

- Engage in activities you are passionate about. Pursuing hobbies can provide a sense of accomplishment and joy.

- Stay informed but avoid excessive exposure to distressing news. Set designated times to catch up on current events.

- Watch a comedy show, read a funny book, or spend time with people who make you laugh. Laughter can reduce stress.

- Practice yoga or gentle stretching to improve flexibility, release tension, and promote relaxation.

- Use guided imagery exercises to create calming mental scenes. Visualization can help reduce stress and anxiety.

- Learn to say no to commitments that overwhelm you. Establish healthy boundaries to prevent burnout.

Remember that caring for yourself is not a selfish act—it is something that every single human needs to do, and by making time to engage with self-care, you are healing your mind and body in subtle ways.

Mindfulness and Grounding Techniques for Promoting Recovery

Mindfulness and grounding techniques can be incredibly effective for promoting recovery from stress, anxiety, trauma, or other challenging experiences. In this section, I'll highlight some of my favorite mindfulness and grounding exercises that you can take into your own healing process.

Let's start with mindfulness. Mindfulness involves awareness over the present moment, including your thoughts, feelings, and present location. Mindfulness can be immensely beneficial for those who experience PTSD because it is a disorder that often leaves us trapped within our own heads. Here are some mindfulness exercises that can help:

- Breath awareness: Focus your attention on your breath. Notice the sensation of each inhale and exhale without trying to change it.

- Body scan: Slowly scan your body from head to toe, paying attention to any sensations or areas of tension. This helps you become aware of how your body is feeling.

- Observing thoughts: Observe your thoughts without judgment. Imagine them as clouds passing by in the sky, allowing them to come and go without clinging to them.

- Sensory awareness: Engage your senses fully in the present moment. Notice the sights, sounds, smells, tastes, and textures around you.

- Eating mindfully: Pay full attention to your eating experience. Savor each bite, notice the flavors and textures, and eat without distractions.

- Mindful walking: Take a slow walk and focus on the sensation of your feet touching the ground. Pay attention to the movement of your body with each step.

- Loving-kindness meditation: Send feelings of compassion and well-wishes to yourself and others. Repeat phrases like "May I be happy, may I be healthy" to cultivate kindness.

In addition, grounding can help draw you back to the present moment, which can be done with these activities:

- 5-4-3-2-1 technique: Name five things you can see, four things you can touch, three things you can hear, two things you can smell, and one thing you can taste.

- Grounding through senses: Engage each of your senses to anchor yourself. Touch something rough or smooth, listen to soothing sounds, taste something flavorful, etc.

- Physical self-touch: Gently touch your arms, legs, or face. Focus on the sensation of touch and the connection between your body and mind.

- Barefoot walking: Walk barefoot on grass, sand, or any natural surface. Pay attention to the textures and sensations under your feet.

- Object exploration: Take an everyday object and examine it closely. Notice its colors, shapes, and textures. This shifts your focus away from distressing thoughts.

- Breathing count: Inhale and exhale slowly while counting each breath. For example, count to four while inhaling, hold for four, and exhale for four.

- Safe place visualization: Close your eyes and imagine a safe, calming place. Describe it in detail, incorporating all your senses.

- Letter or word focus: Choose a word or letter and find it in your surroundings. This simple activity redirects your attention to the present moment.

Living with PTSD can be really hard, and that difficulty is only compounded if you are not sure what your triggers are or how you can identify them. Now, however, you have the tools necessary to not only identify your triggers, but to manage, handle, and overcome them as well. This is a major step forward in your PTSD recovery, and for that, I commend you!

Chapter 7:
Fostering Healthy Relationships and Support Systems

Each of us has the power to inspire or depress, to lift others or to push them down. —Wilferd Peterson

During the process of recovering and being kind to myself after traumatic events, support systems and healthy relationships have been invaluable. It was my friends, family, and others who helped me get through some of the rougher parts of my life, and I know that's the case for others as well. Whether you know who you can rely on now or you are starting from ground zero with developing the support system of your dreams, I'm here to help. Do not worry—you do not have to do anything as of this second; I'll guide you every step of the way. This chapter will focus on the importance of healthy relationships to your recovery, strategies for improving your communication and trust in a relationship, what you can do to establish healthy boundaries, and so much more. If you are ready to take the first baby steps into building the support network of your dreams, then let's get started!

The Importance of Healthy Relationships in PTSD Recovery

I cannot even begin to count the number of people that I've met who think they can go at it alone, recovering from their PTSD and its symptoms without any support from others at all. I'm sure someone somewhere has accomplished that feat, but it is not the norm in the slightest; rather, a lot of people need support from others, and in fact, there are myriad reasons why you should seek out support in the first place.

One reason that safe, healthy relationships are important to the process of PTSD recovery is that they provide us with emotional support. Healthy relationships provide us with a safe space through which we can express our thoughts and feelings without judgment. Having someone who listens and understands can help reduce feelings of isolation and loneliness. If you have ever gone to a friend to vent and were offered a shoulder to cry on or even some really good advice, then you know exactly what I mean!

In addition, it is important to foster healthy relationships because they provide us with validation and understanding. Especially in the case of loved ones who understand PTSD as a disorder, our support networks can provide us with validation of our experiences that can counter feelings of self-doubt and helplessness often associated with trauma. Moreover, it can be easy to feel like no one on Earth understands what we're going through when it comes to PTSD and trauma. By forming a support network, you might find that more people than you had thought are acquainted with what trauma is and what it is like to have traumatic experiences. This can make you feel even more understood!

Furthermore, a support network can help reduce the isolation you may be feeling. PTSD can lead to withdrawal and social isolation, and healthy relationships encourage engagement with the world, reducing feelings of detachment and helping individuals reconnect with others. When you develop and engage with a support group, you interact with other people and push those feelings of social isolation away. This is a fantastic benefit because isolation can also often exacerbate certain symptoms of PTSD, like paranoia and anxiety.

Another benefit of having a support group for PTSD recovery is that a support network can lessen the amount of stress that you feel. Supportive relationships provide emotional stability, reducing the impact of stress and anxiety that can exacerbate PTSD symptoms. Those who support us can take some tasks off of our hands, making it easier to function, or just provide us with much needed emotional support that can relieve stress. Either way, it is beneficial to be less stressed out when you have a disorder with "stress" in the name!

Other benefits of having a support group for PTSD recovery include:

- Healthy relationships can offer practical coping strategies for managing PTSD symptoms. Loved ones can provide reassurance, distraction, and assistance in applying relaxation techniques.

- Being in relationships where others are aware of PTSD symptoms can help normalize these reactions. This normalization can ease self-criticism and promote acceptance.

- Supportive relationships can encourage individuals to seek professional treatment for PTSD. Loved ones can provide encouragement and logistical support in accessing therapy and treatment.

- PTSD can erode trust in oneself and others. Healthy relationships based on trust and mutual respect contribute to the gradual rebuilding of trust.

- Positive relationships foster a sense of worth and self-esteem. This, in turn, supports the individual's overall healing journey.

- As recovery progresses, supportive relationships can provide feedback on positive changes and growth. Celebrating milestones can reinforce the individual's sense of achievement.

- Healthy relationships provide a sense of belonging and connection. This can counter feelings of detachment that often accompany PTSD.

- Trusted loved ones can provide a sense of safety, which can help reduce hypervigilance and anxiety that are common in PTSD.

- Being around supportive individuals can motivate individuals with PTSD to engage in social activities, reducing avoidance behavior.

- Trusted friends and family can offer an outside perspective on situations, helping individuals challenge distorted thinking patterns common in PTSD.

- Healthy relationships can serve as models for healthy communication and interactions. Learning from these relationships can improve the individual's overall communication skills.

- Supportive individuals can help buffer the impact of trauma triggers by offering reassurance and guidance during difficult moments.

It is not uncommon for someone with PTSD to have experienced relationship-related trauma, and even if you do not have that experience, it can still be hard to make friends and connections that are kind and supportive. Do not worry; the ensuing sections will go over what you can do to facilitate these connections in depth.

Strategies for Improving Communication and Trust

Communication and trust are two points of relationships that can be particularly difficult for PTSD survivors. It can be hard, but there are different strategies that you can employ in order to help yourself—and those you talk to—form communication habits and trust for one another that facilitate strong relationships.

Improving Communication

Improving communication is easier than it seems. Here's what you can do to improve your communication skills in order to foster strong relationships that help you through this moment:

- Pay close attention to what the other person is saying, and show that you are engaged by nodding, making eye contact, and asking relevant questions.

- Use questions that require more than a simple yes or no answer. This encourages the other person to share their thoughts and feelings more deeply.

- Clarify misunderstandings by asking for clarification rather than assuming you know what the other person means.

- Express your thoughts and feelings using "I" statements, which can help prevent blame and defensiveness. For example, say "I felt hurt when..." instead of "You hurt me when...".

- Show empathy by acknowledging the other person's emotions and validating their experiences, even if you do not agree.

- Put away distractions when communicating. Being fully present shows that you value the conversation.

- Summarize what you have understood from the conversation and ask if you got it right. This confirms your understanding and gives the other person a chance to clarify if needed.

- Choose the right time to have important conversations. Avoid discussing sensitive topics when either party is tired, stressed, or preoccupied.

- Pay attention to your body language, tone of voice, and facial expressions. They convey a lot about your emotions and intentions.

By working with these tactics for improved communication, you are sure to foster stronger relationships within your support network.

Improving Trust

When it comes to PTSD, trust can be particularly challenging. However, these tips will help you foster trust between you and others:

- Follow through on your promises and commitments. Being consistent builds trust over time.

- Be open about your thoughts, feelings, and intentions. Avoid hidden agendas or secrets that could erode trust.

- Acknowledge when you have made a mistake, and take responsibility for your actions. This demonstrates accountability.

- Honor the other person's boundaries and communicate your own. This shows that you value and respect their comfort zones.

- Sharing your vulnerabilities and challenges can create a deeper connection and show that you are willing to be authentic.

- Approach situations without preconceived judgments. Creating a judgment-free zone fosters trust.

- When someone apologizes or makes amends, practice forgiveness. Holding onto grudges can damage trust.

- Offer encouragement and support for the other person's goals and endeavors. This shows that you are invested in their success.

- Clearly communicate your expectations and boundaries. Clarity helps prevent misunderstandings that could undermine trust.

- Respect the other person's need for space and independence. Trust involves giving each other room to grow.

- Celebrate each other's achievements, no matter how small. Positive reinforcement strengthens trust and positive associations.

Remember that improving communication and trust is an ongoing process that requires patience, effort, and active participation from all parties involved. These strategies can help create a strong foundation for healthier, more fulfilling relationships, and as a result, your PTSD symptoms may abate.

Establishing Boundaries and Nurturing Supportive Relationships

For any strong, supportive relationship, boundaries are necessary. Boundaries are limitations that we place upon ourselves and others to make ourselves feel safe and respected. And believe it or not, in just eight steps, you can set strong boundaries that are unmoving and helpful for you. Here are those steps:

1. Understand your own needs, values, and comfort levels. This awareness is essential for setting effective boundaries.

2. Determine what behaviors, actions, or situations make you uncomfortable or stressed. These will help define your boundaries.

3. Express your boundaries directly and assertively. Use "I" statements to convey your needs without blaming or criticizing.

4. Begin by setting boundaries in less challenging situations. Gradually expand them to more significant areas of your life.

5. Once you have established boundaries, consistently enforce them. This reinforces your commitment to your own well-being.

6. Show respect for the boundaries of others, just as you expect them to respect yours.

7. Boundaries might change based on circumstances or personal growth. Be open to adjusting them when necessary.

8. Maintain your boundaries as a form of self-care. Remember that setting limits helps protect your mental and emotional health.

Not only do boundaries keep us safe, but they foster strong relationships. Develop your boundaries to foster these strong relationships!

Healing From Relationship Trauma and Fostering Connection

When it comes to PTSD, it is all too common that relationship trauma coexists. All hope is not lost when it comes to that relationship trauma, though—there are ways that you can heal from that relationship trauma in order to foster connection between you and those around you for strong relationships. Here are some of the tips that helped me the most when it came to healing from my own relationship trauma:

- A therapist experienced in trauma and relationship issues can provide a safe space for you to process your emotions and develop coping strategies.

- Be kind to yourself. Treat yourself as you would treat a close friend going through a difficult time.

- A therapist experienced in trauma and relationship issues can provide a safe space for you to process your emotions and develop coping strategies.

- Establish clear boundaries in all your relationships. This empowers you to protect your emotional well-being.

- Reflect on patterns in your past relationships. Recognizing recurring behaviors can help you make more informed choices in the future.

- Understand your triggers, needs, and vulnerabilities. Self-awareness can guide your interactions and choices.

- Healing takes time. Be patient with yourself and allow yourself to gradually process and heal from the trauma.

- Learn healthy ways to manage your emotions. Techniques like mindfulness, deep breathing, and grounding can be helpful.

- Prioritize self-care activities that promote your well-being, whether it is exercise, creative pursuits, nature walks, or relaxation techniques.

- Write about your thoughts and feelings. Journaling can help you gain clarity, express yourself, and track your progress.

- Surround yourself with individuals who are understanding, empathetic, and supportive of your healing journey.

- When you are ready, share your experience with trusted individuals who can provide validation and comfort.

- As you forge new relationships, take your time in building trust. Allow trust to develop organically.

- Work on your communication skills to express your needs, set boundaries, and resolve conflicts in a healthy manner.

- Channel your energy into personal growth and self-improvement. Rediscover your passions and strengths.

- Forgiveness does not mean condoning the behavior. It is about releasing the emotional burden for your own well-being.

- Remember that healing from relationship trauma is an opportunity for growth and a chance to build more authentic, fulfilling connections in the future.

Now that you have what you need to foster healthy relationships, you can build the support group you need in order to heal and recover from PTSD. It might seem scary at first, but over time you can find your footing and strong relationships that benefit you for the rest of your life.

Chapter 8:
Managing Sleep and Nightmares

Do not fight with the pillow, but lay down your head, and kick every worriment out of the bed. —Elie Wiesel, Night

It is surprising to me just how many people undervalue sleep. Sleep is the body's time to rest and recharge, both healing and processing information from the day prior. Our body does so much work at night, that it is a wonder we wake up feeling rested at all. However, for someone with PTSD, you might *not* wake up rested at all—the nightmares and night terrors, insomnia, fear, and other symptoms can pose a true issue for you when you lay down your head at night. That's something I understand all too well.

In fact, I wrote an entire book on my experience with insomnia and how it plagued me—as well as what I did to overcome it. "Insomnia Solutions" is one of my first books, and I truly recommend it if you are interested in diving deeper into the contents of this chapter. When I was first experiencing insomnia-related PTSD, it was a frustrating experience to say the least. But now, I have the power to recognize it as the gift that it was, allowing me to grow and heal. Let's help you get to that point too.

The Impact of Sleep on PTSD Symptoms

The impact that sleep has on PTSD symptoms—and vice versa—cannot go unnoticed. Understanding this link is important; right now, you might be experiencing a number of symptoms or a worsening in symptoms, all due to your sleep habits. Understanding the impact that sleep has on PTSD and the impact that PTSD can have on sleep is vital to ensuring that you can identify where this link shows up in your life. Once you can, you have the power to remedy it. So, let's talk about the impact of sleep on PTSD.

To start, did you know that those with insomnia or other significant sleep problems are statistically more likely to develop PTSD (How Post-Traumatic Stress Disorder Affects Sleep, 2020)? I did not know this, and when I found out, a few things made sense! It is also the case that sleep disturbances often manifest as the first symptoms of PTSD. Whether it be night terrors, insomnia, or the ability to attain deep and restful sleep, PTSD often impacts our sleep-life first.

In tandem, sleep can also make PTSD symptoms worse. If you do not get enough good quality sleep every single night, you might experience a significant worsening in your symptoms. Just a fraction of the ways that sleep can impact your PTSD symptoms includes:

- Nightmares and flashbacks. At night, when you are lying down and trying to shut your mind off, it is no wonder that you may be susceptible to nightmares and flashbacks. In fact, flashbacks are a hallmark symptom of PTSD, and nighttime can often be the most common time for symptoms like nightmares, flashbacks, or intrusive thoughts to occur. This can often lead one to wake up in a state of distress, further promoting symptoms of anxiety and/or hypervigilance.

- Poor sleep quality. A common affliction for those who have PTSD is the inability to fall asleep and stay asleep. As a result, poor sleep quality can plague those with PTSD, leading to waking up often, tossing and turning, and struggling to reach truly deep stages of sleep. In turn, this can lead to increased irritability, fatigue, and difficulty concentrating, all of which are common PTSD symptoms.

- Hyperarousal. Most people who have PTSD are no strangers to hyperarousal. Hyperarousal is a state that is often characterized by a heightened fight-or-flight response to various stimuli, and sleep disturbances can make this symptom of PTSD worse. This, in turn, can make it rather difficult for those with PTSD to relax or feel safe at bedtime, leading to increased stress and anxiety.

- Impaired emotional regulation. Did you know that sleep is actually crucial for emotional regulation? Not getting enough sleep at night can result in challenges with managing emotions and coping with distressing memories that are associated with trauma. As a result, this can lead to heightened anger, depression, or anxiety, or the inability to control those emotions.

- Difficulty consolidating memories. Sleep is the time during which the brain consolidates and processes our memories. Disrupted sleep can make it challenging for the brain to consolidate memories pertaining to trauma, which in some cases can make these memories more intrusive and pervasive.

- Physical health issues. Immune function and inflammation are just two of the many physical health impacts that stem from not getting enough sleep. Physical health issues can cause increased stress, making it hard to manage PTSD symptoms.

And that's certainly not all, either. Knowing this, you might feel compelled to understand how you can improve your sleep and the connection between sleep and PTSD. I know I was when I first found out. Do not worry; the coming sections center themselves around truly helping you obtain the best quality of sleep possible, despite the challenges that may arise as a result of your disorder.

Improving Sleep Quality and Establishing a Routine

Now that you understand some of the most impactful roles that sleep can have on PTSD, you are probably wondering just what exactly can be done to fix this. After all, sleep is essential regardless of if you have PTSD, and many people have problems with sleep as is. Fixing your sleep habits might feel like an uphill battle, but by taking the three-pronged approach of sleep hygiene, bedtime routine, and avoiding certain items before bed, you can improve both the quality and duration of your sleep. This will also improve your mental and physical health, making it easier to manage PTSD symptoms. Let's start by unveiling sleep hygiene.

Sleep Hygiene Techniques

Sleep hygiene is not what it sounds like; it is not about sleeping in clean sheets and pajamas every night, after taking a bubble bath and so on. Although these things may be able to help improve the quality of your sleep in some respects, that's not what sleep hygiene is all about. Rather, sleep hygiene refers to a set of habits that, when employed, can help you sleep better. Following good sleep hygiene is proven to improve sleep quality as well as overall well-being, which makes a compelling case for why you should engage with it.

There are several different components of maintaining good sleep hygiene that you should be aware of. Do not worry if you cannot achieve all of these aspects overnight; even small but consistent changes build up to make a difference. The first aspect of engaging with sleep hygiene is to develop a consistent sleep schedule. It can be tempting to sleep in on weekends or stay up late on nights you do not have to be up early the following day, but by waking up and going to bed at the same times every night, you help your body's clock regulate itself. Doing so allows your brain to know when it is time to rest, helping it to shut off those disturbing or intrusive thoughts when bedtime rolls around. Instead, your brain will associate bedtime with rest and relaxation.

The next aspect of sleep hygiene that you should be aware of involves creating a sleep environment for yourself that feels comfortable and safe. If you have ever slept on a couch for a night, then you know just how much being comfortable where you sleep matters. There are a few different aspects of creating a comfortable sleep environment for yourself. For starters, your pillows and mattress matter. By investing in a high quality mattress and comfortable pillows for your body, you will get far better rest. You should also be mindful of the temperature that you keep your bedroom. Statistically, keeping your room in the 60-69 degree Fahrenheit range is perfect for optimal sleep conditions. Finally, it is vital to make sure that your room is both dark and quiet when you sleep. Some people feel as though they need noise or light for sleep and therefore opt for the TV, but I recommend a white noise machine or Himalayan salt lamp for those needs.

Another good way to ensure sleep hygiene is to pay attention to the things that you do before bed. For example, you should try to avoid using screens, including phones, computers, and TVs, starting an hour before bedtime. A lot of people think a blue light filter can counteract the effect that screens have on our circadian rhythm cycles, but they do not; altogether avoiding screen time is going to give you the best results. In addition, you should avoid stimulants before bed. Caffeine and alcohol are two common stimulants that can keep you up or harm your sleep cycle. I also recommend avoiding heavy or spicy foods before bedtime, as the digestive process is a lot harsher for these foods and can keep you up.

Moreover, it is an excellent idea to limit the amount of naps you take. At first, this is going to be a really hard process. I used to take naps all the time because of insomnia, but at the end of the day—literally and figuratively—napping kept me up at night, which only perpetuated the cycle. If staying away is genuinely a struggle, I recommend slowly going to bed earlier in the day and then pushing that bedtime until it is where you want it to be; that way, at least you get decent quality sleep rather than staggered naps.

Finally, I recommend ensuring that you get enough sunlight exposure. It might not seem like it would do a lot, but the natural rays of sunlight are your body's way of regulating its clock. By getting even 10-20 minutes of sunlight exposure, especially in the morning, you can help your body regulate its sleep-wake cycles for more comfortable sleep at night. I have more on this and other sleep hygiene tips in "Insomnia Solutions."

So to recap, key techniques for improving your sleep hygiene include:

- Consistent sleep schedule

- Making your sleep environment comfortable

- Limiting exposure to certain substances and items

- Limit napping

- Get enough sunlight

Sleep hygiene is an important skill set for all PTSD survivors to have. Not only does it entire the quality and quantity of your rest, but it can help fend off some of the more discomforting symptoms of PTSD all the while.

Establishing a Comforting Bedtime Routine

Another option that you have for enhancing your ability to get enough good quality sleep is to establish a comforting bedtime routine. In order to establish a bedtime routine, I always say it involves three steps.

The first step is pre-bedtime preparation. This consists of all of the things that you need to do prior to getting ready for bed. I always recommend a few actions for your pre-bedtime preparation:

- Shut off all electronics. If you need an alarm for the next morning, set it now and leave your phone alone.

- Crank down the AC for your bedtime oasis—remember that the ideal temperature is 60-67 degrees Fahrenheit.

- Put on some comfy sleepwear.

- Have a light snack and some water if you need it.

After you have made those preparations, you can proceed to the next step. Remember not to skip these aspects, because they'll help you maintain good sleep hygiene to get the rest you need in order to heal.

Then, there's the relaxation step. This is the step that involves winding down for bedtime before you actually go to sleep. During this step, you can do whatever you want as long as it is relaxing and soothing. This will help your mind get into sleep mode. Some of my favorite activities for the relaxation step of my bedtime routine are reading, praying, and coloring. Adult coloring books are soothing alternatives to watching TV or movies if you want something more creative to do, and reading can slow you down. And of course, prayer helps with the spiritual aspects of sleep if that's within your belief system.

Finally, you have to actually go to bed. Put down your activity of choice, dim the lights or turn them off entirely, and get into bed. With your relaxing bedtime routine, you should be able to get more rest. Even if it does not work the first night, falling into the routine over and over will eventually help your mind find peace and calm for rest.

Coping With Nightmares and Night Terrors

Nightmares and night terrors are two incredibly common symptoms of PTSD. They're symptoms that not only disturb sleep greatly, but lead to worsening of other symptoms like hypervigilance and anxiety as well. By understanding nightmares and night terrors, as well as how to manage them, you can learn to get more restful sleep despite these obstacles.

What's the Difference?

A lot of people wrongly conflate nightmares and night terrors. While both can be symptoms that arise from PTSD, understanding the difference is key to your recovery. Let's talk about the difference.

Nightmares are often described as vivid yet disturbing dreams. They center themselves around distressing circumstances and can cause fear, anxiety, and similar emotions. With nightmares, it is usually the case that someone can remember their nightmare once they wake up. They occur when vivid dreaming occurs in the rapid eye movement stage of sleep, which is a deep level of sleep that a lot of individuals with PTSD struggle to attain. While experiencing a nightmare, you might sweat, find your heart rate increases, or pant in response to the psychological distress.

Night terrors are a completely different story. Night terrors are episodic and intense levels of fear that occur during sleep, but they do not involve dreams or nightmares. Instead, there is often no memory associated with the event, and it can occur early in the night or sleep cycle. There are often more physical signs than nightmares, including complex movements, screaming, and thrashing about. It is very hard to comfort someone from a night terror.

Many individuals who experience PTSD have nightmares or night terrors, and in some unfortunate cases, both co-exist. Understanding how to cope with either or both is valuable and allows one to avoid losing out on valuable hours of sleep. Let's uncover what can be done in order to assist with coping with nightmares and night terrors.

One of the most important skills that you can foster when it comes to overcoming PTSD is how to cope with nightmares and night terrors that can accompany the disorder. Depending on whether you personally experience nightmares or night terrors, there are going to be different solutions for you. For example, some methods of coping with nightmares include:

- Identifying triggers. Of course, your PTSD and trauma are going to serve as triggers, but see if you can determine other instances where your nightmares are triggered by daily events, actions, and circumstances. If you can pick up on a certain pattern, then you know what to avoid when it comes to triggers.

- Improve your sleep hygiene. As mentioned in the previous section, improving your sleep hygiene can make a significant impact on the quality and quantity of your sleep. Did you know that sleep hygiene can also prevent nightmares? It can! By ensuring that you engage with strong sleep hygiene practices, you can prevent nightmares in their tracks.

- Make use of relaxation techniques. The next section centers itself around several relaxation techniques that you can employ for better rest. Using those techniques prior to bedtime can reduce nightmares, and using them when and if a nightmare occurs can be helpful as well.

- Limit your media exposure. Every day, we are exposed to violent or disheartening content online. Limit your exposure to media that does not add positivity to your life, and you will probably notice that you have less nightmares as well.

Furthermore, some methods to help you cope with night terrors include:

- Safety precautions. If you know that you are prone to night terrors, removing sharp or unsafe objects from the sleeping area can keep you safe in the event that a night terror takes place.

- Relaxation techniques. Like with nightmares, the relaxation techniques of the next chapter can be particularly helpful in reducing how often night terrors occur as well as how intense they are.

- Stick to a regular sleep schedule. A regular sleep schedule can serve to calm your body down and keep you more peaceful overnight.

This can help reduce the frequency of night terrors in your life.

- Limit alcohol and caffeine consumption. Studies have linked substance use, including alcohol and caffeine, to increased night terrors. This means that you can reduce the frequency with which night terrors impact you by reducing your caffeine and alcohol intake.

- Medication and therapy. If your night terrors become severe enough, it might be necessary to seek professional help in order to manage the symptoms of your night terrors.

One common coping mechanism to both nightmares and night terrors was relaxation techniques. Now, we're going to talk about relaxation techniques that can help you cope not just with nightmares and night terrors, but empower you to overcome all manner of sleep-related symptoms as well.

Relaxation Techniques for Rest

I cannot stress enough the importance of a good relaxation technique when it comes to the intersection between PTSD and sleep. Not only can being overly stressed out prevent sleep in and of itself, but stress is linked to intense physical side effects that can impact the quality of your rest. I have first-hand experience with the link between stress and physical pain, as well as how that stress can manifest into a lack of sleep.

As I said, stress can transform itself into physical pain. This is all the more reason to combat stress as soon as humanly possible.

With all of that being said, the importance of relaxation for your well-being is crucial. This section provides you with tons of the most effective relaxation techniques—ones that have helped thousands of people with PTSD—that you can use in order to sleep better.

Progressive Muscle Relaxation

The first relaxation method that I want to share with you is progressive muscle relaxation. I know that after I endured significant trauma, I was prone to holding excess tension throughout my body. The same is probably true for you. Progressive muscle relaxation is going to be best done in bed or otherwise lying down, and it involves relaxing the entire body, one area at a time. You're going to start at the bottom with your toes. Begin by releasing any tension you are holding there, relaxing your feet, ankles, and then moving up into your calves. Continue going up the body, relaxing each component until you get all the way to your head and face. As a result of this activity, you will probably recognize that you have been tensed up or holding tension without meaning to.

Deep Breathing

Hyperventilation and other breathing problems are not uncommon to those with PTSD. Practicing deep breathing before bed or in specific times of stress can be especially helpful, because it is known to relax your mind and body as well as promote more restful sleep. In order to engage with deep breathing, follow these steps:

1. Find a quiet, comfortable place to sit or lie down.

2. Close your eyes and take a slow, deep breath in through your nose, counting to four.

3. Hold your breath for a count of four.

4. Exhale slowly through your mouth for a count of six.

Repeat these four simple steps over and over until you feel more relaxed and calmer.

Guided Imagery and Visualization

Another method for relaxing before bed that I want to share with you is guided imagery and visualization. There are numerous videos on YouTube and other apps like Headspace that can guide you through gorgeous scenic meditations in order to calm you down. You do not even have to meditate for a long period of time—even five minutes a day can make a major difference. With meditation, it is always helpful to remember that consistency is more important than duration.

Other Relaxation Methods

There are hundreds of other methods that you can use to relax before bedtime. Just to share a few more:

- Aromatherapy. Making use of essential oils in a diffuser, bath, or on your pillow can calm you down due to the fact that certain scents trigger calming sensations in the brain.

- Warm bath. Taking a warm bath, especially with Epsom salts or oils in the bath, can help you relax and get ready for bed.

- Stretching. Light yoga or other forms of stretching can be a great way to release tension from your body and get ready for bed.

- Reading. Reading can take your mind off of worries and reduce stress—and yes, audiobooks work too. Just be mindful of what you choose to fill your head space with, especially before bed!

- Journaling. If anything is troubling you or on your mind, writing it down before bed can help clear your mind and reduce those pesky racing thoughts.

Getting enough sleep is important. Without sleep, your mind, body, and soul cannot heal or be at their best. But now, you know how to improve your quality of rest overall, even with the obstacles that PTSD can impose. How awesome is that?

Chapter 9:
Self-Care and Stress Management

You are imperfect, you are wired for struggle, but you are worthy of love and belonging. —Brené Brown

I cannot even begin to tell you how many people I know who think self-care is overrated. It is not all about bubble baths and cute walks through the park—although those can definitely be self-care activities for some people. Rather, self-care is a valuable and essential tool that makes a major difference in the healing process, but do not take it from me; let's start the chapter off with some science-backed reasons that self-care is crucial to PTSD recovery.

The Importance of Self-Care to PTSD Recovery

Can you name three ways that self-care is important to PTSD recovery? If not, that's okay—I can name way more than three, all of which are backed by research, and I'm going to share those with you right now. Here are 10 fabulous ways that self-care benefits the PTSD recovery process:

1. Reduced stress and anxiety. It is not called post-traumatic *stress* disorder for no reason; stress and heightened levels of anxiety often accompany PTSD, which is why self-care is such a compelling part of recovery. Self-care has the striking ability to reduce the amount of stress and anxiety felt by those with PTSD through something as simple as doing things you love that feel kind and rewarding.

2. Improved coping skills. That's right; self-care can actually help you better cope with the triggers and symptoms involved in PTSD. Healthy coping mechanisms like setting boundaries, problem solving, seeking support, and more can all empower your coping skills tool box, and they're also all part of self-care.

3. Enhanced emotional regulation. Those with PTSD can struggle with their sense of emotional regulation, which is why it is such a good thing that self-care can actually supercharge your ability to regulate your emotions. This is because activities that bring you joy and can help you express your emotions in a healthy way—like art, journaling, and more—can all help you regulate and understand

what you feel.

4. Improved sleep. Practicing self-care including methods like good sleep hygiene can truly make it easier for you to fall asleep, stay asleep, and wake up feeling well rested.

5. Less isolation. Self-care activities often involve finding a support group and connecting to others. This can reduce the feelings of isolation and withdrawal that often accompany PTSD and similar disorders.

6. Improved self-esteem. Taking the time to care for yourself shows yourself that you are worth love and respect, which counteracts some of the negative self-perceptions that accompany PTSD.

7. Improved physical health. Physical activity is often a part of self-care. By engaging in regular physical activity, you can care for yourself while reducing some of the impacts of PTSD.

8. Less hypervigilance. Hypervigilance is a common symptom of PTSD that can make you tired and stressed; however, by caring for yourself, you can engage with relaxation that lowers hypervigilance and allows you to rest.

9. Increased resilience. Self-care can enable you to better cope with stressors and triggers associated with PTSD.

10. Enhanced treatment outcomes. By taking good care of yourself, your medication, therapy, and other treatments will be vastly more successful.

Evidently, there are plenty of ways to engage with self-care for PTSD recovery. Let's dive into some of those methods.

Strategies for Managing Stress and Anxiety

Managing stress and anxiety is one aspect of self-care to be mindful of. You can engage with the following activities for managing your stress and anxiety:

- Deep breathing. Earlier, I mentioned an exercise for deep breathing that can help you sleep. As it turns out, deep breathing is also good for helping you manage your stress and anxiety for PTSD recovery.

- Mindfulness meditation. Mindfulness guided meditations are all over the internet, and they can help you manage stress and anxiety. It is easy for mindfulness meditation to help with stress and anxiety because they take our mind off of some of the overwhelming parts of life and instead allow us to focus on the present moment.

- Progressive muscle relaxation. Those who experience stress and anxiety hold significant amounts of tension in the body, which can lead to increased symptoms. Practicing the muscle relaxation methods we talked about earlier will help you out significantly.

- Exercise. Most notably, exercise can reduce the amount of cortisol—a stress hormone—in your body, replacing it instead with the pleasure-facilitating endorphins.

- Limiting stimulant and alcohol usage. Alcohol and other substances can cause increased stress and anxiety due to how they interact with our bodily systems; a good method of self-care, then, is to avoid these substances.

- Task management. By working hard to manage your tasks throughout the day, you can decrease the amount of overall stress that you feel as the day goes by. While this may not help with PTSD per se, it can certainly be an overlooked part of decreasing stress.

- Journaling. Journaling can be a wonderful manner in which to relieve stress by "talking" about some of the things that are bothering you. I recommend making journaling a habit for the best results.

Remember that stress and anxiety management are valuable components of self-care that can truly make your life—and symptoms—easier to manage. It can be easy to say "oh, I'll just deal with it," when it comes to stress, but that's certainly not the way to go.

Infusing Self-Care Into Daily Life

Finding time for self-care can be really hard. As a mother, a CEO, and otherwise just a very busy person, I know that I struggle to find time for self-care every day. But despite that, I fight to make the time, because I know just how important self-care can be. Especially when you are first starting out, infusing self-care into your daily life can seem like a tall order; that's why I have some tips for you to infuse self-care into your life without added stress or strain, helping your symptoms improve all the while.

First, it is important to start with small steps. Consistency is far more important than duration; even working with self-care for five minutes a day can make major improvements. I recommend finding a spot in your existing routine where you could take 5-10 minutes for yourself, and then dedicating that time for self-care. It is one of the ways that I've personally been able to infuse self-care into my very busy schedule, even if it is as simple as stretching, having a snack, or going for a walk.

Setting boundaries is also an important part of self-care that many people forget about. Boundaries are restrictions that we place upon ourselves or others to ensure that we receive proper treatment. Boundaries are, therefore, of the essence for someone recovering from PTSD. Do not be afraid to say "no" when you need to. Communicate your boundaries openly and clearly, and refuse to let others push them around—trust me, it may be hard, but it will be one of the best changes you can make for your recovery.

In addition, taking five minutes to keep up with a gratitude journal is not only an amazing way to infuse self-care into the day, but it also reminds us that there's more to life than the doom and gloom our disorder can convince us of. Just try to get into the habit of writing down 3-5 things that you are grateful for every day, and you will notice strong improvements in how happy you are with life.

On your journey to PTSD recovery, learning to love, trust, and care for yourself gently and compassionately is a vital step forward in order to truly heal. With what you have learned in this chapter, you have the ability to overcome some of the most destructive feelings that you might have toward yourself, beginning to truly embrace yourself as the wonderful person you are. Good work!

Chapter 10:
Building a Meaningful and Purposeful Life

If your compassion does not include yourself, it is incomplete. —Jack Kornfield

It is true—you cannot truly be compassionate if you do not care for yourself as well as those around you. One of the best ways that you can be compassionate to yourself is taking the time to build a meaningful and purposeful life after trauma. One of the biggest issues that I hear trauma survivors mention is that life lacks zest, purpose, and meaning. Let's not live that way—life is too beautiful of a gift to waste it wondering about what our purpose is and what meaning it should have.

Finding Purpose and Meaning After Trauma

Finding purpose and meaning after enduring a traumatic event can be one of the hardest things to do. Trauma often makes it feel like we've been stripped of our purpose, that there's nothing left for us and that the meaning of life is for us to suffer. This is not true at all. I personally found purpose and meaning in the Lord and my religion after trauma, which has been an endless gift that I am so grateful for. Alongside religion, or without it if that's your preferred lifestyle, there are plenty of ways that you can reinforce purpose and meaning in your life.

Think about something that you are passionate about, or even something that matters to you just a little. Maybe you think art conservation is important, or pet shelters are one of the best things on Earth. Maybe it is something as simple as loving iced coffee. Think about just one thing that you care for in some way and allow that to be your jumping off point. Make it a habit to incorporate that thing into your life; it does not have to become your whole life, but by starting there, you cannot say your life is "meaningless"—which is a big step forward in progressing your mindset.

You can make it a habit to volunteer, socialize, or otherwise act to bring you closer to that thing of value. Overtime, your values might change, your interests will shift, and you might want to spend some time focusing on other things—that's okay! Life is all about change and growth. On your journey to recovering from PTSD, it is going to be essential to set goals that help you achieve more in life, no matter how big or small. Let's talk about how we can set meaningful goals that drive us toward achievement.

Goal Setting and Pursuing Passions

Goal setting is one way that we can work toward pursuing our passions and finding meaning after trauma. Not only do goals keep us focused on what we want to achieve, but they also provide us with structured landmarks against which we can review progress and see how far we've come. There are hundreds, maybe even thousands, of methods for goal setting. However, my favorite one is SMART goal setting, which is also the most approved method of goal setting around.

The first step in setting a SMART goal is that your goal must be specific. For example, if you want to set a goal to keep up with a journal, you're going to need to get a little more specific. Setting a goal to "journal" is good, but setting a goal to "journal for 15 minutes every day" is *great!* This is because a specific goal both keeps you accountable and leaves no room for interpretation, which in turn makes sure that you're actually making the progress that you want to make.

Something else to keep in mind is that your SMART goal must be measurable. Most goals are inherently measurable, but this also means that you have to specify a measure upon which you'll consider the goal to be a success. For example, keeping with the journaling example, the "measure" for that goal would be to journal for 15 minutes a day. You can get even more specific with how you measure your goal, but it's essential to measure it in some way that is meaningful to you.

The next consideration for a SMART goal is that it must be attainable. You can't set a goal for yourself that is purely impossible; or, rather, you can, but it won't do you any good. Setting goals that aren't attainable will only serve to demotivate you. On the other hand, setting goals that are truly within your reach can be inspiring and motivational, creating a desire within you to seek out more from life. When you set attainable goals, you keep yourself motivated.

Your SMART goal also has to be relevant. What do I mean by that? Well, simply put, your goal must matter to you and your overall life aspirations. If you set a goal that doesn't matter to you or your recovery in some way, then you're just keeping yourself busy—you're not actually doing something that will better you or your life. However, by setting goals that truly matter to you, you'll not only be motivated to achieve those goals, but

The final aspect of SMART goal setting is to set goals that are time-bound. This simply means putting some form of time restriction on your goal within which you have to complete it; for instance, in the "journal for 15 minutes every day" goal, "everyday" is the time limit. If you don't have time-bound goals, then it's less likely that you'll actually achieve them since you have the ability to endlessly push your goal around.

In some cases, people like to turn SMART goals into SMARTER goals. While the E and R can vary depending on who you as, I like to think of it this way:

- Evaluate. The E stands for evaluate, which means taking the time to decide how your progress has been coming. For example, if you find that you've only been able to journal for 10 minutes a day instead of 15, then that's something to take note of and adapt in the next point, which is...

- Reorient. It's okay to reorient your goals to meet your needs. That "journal for 15 minutes every day" goal can become "journal for 10 minutes every day." That's not a sign of failure; it's a sign of being able to adapt to your needs and be self-aware.

If this goal setting method doesn't work for you, just look up "best goal setting methods." There are so many alternative methods you can explore, and one is bound to work perfectly for your needs.

Help—I Don't Have Passions!

I used to cringe when faced with the question, "What are your interests or hobbies?" It seemed like such an innocuous inquiry, typically asked when getting to know someone. However, for me, it triggered a significant struggle that often resulted in feelings of anxiety. Why? Because I didn't have a clear answer. At my lowest points, it felt unacceptable to admit that my pastime primarily consisted of watching TV and being alone.

I yearned to break free from this negative and unhealthy state of existence. It reached a breaking point when I became utterly fed up with being trapped in this never-ending cycle. It was a friend of mine who suggested I reflect on my childhood, asking myself, "What did I enjoy doing back then?" This led me back to fond memories of summer camp and the joy of participating in arts and crafts, a world that felt light-years away from my current reality.

In those early stages of breaking free from the darkness, my life was primarily composed of sleep and activities that I deemed essential for work—both in terms of career and daily life. Determined to make a change, I took the first step. I purchased some string and started crafting friendship bracelets. I also printed out some "free adult coloring pages" from the internet. To my surprise, these seemingly simple activities proved to be incredibly relaxing and left me with a sense of fulfillment.

With time, I expanded my horizons. I began to notice and appreciate the small wonders of life, like capturing the beauty of nature through photography or even making an effort to present food beautifully on a plate (even if my culinary skills weren't top-notch – but hey, cooking isn't my strong suit!). Photography, in particular, has become an integral part of my life. It allows me to pause and truly see the beauty in the little things, such as a fallen leaf resting on a table. It has been a gradual process, but I've finally reached a point where I can genuinely appreciate the beauty in life once again

Everyone has something they're passionate about, but I understand feeling like you don't. PTSD can bury the things that we care about the most deep within us, making us feel like those passions are pointless or purposeless. If you don't feel like you have any passions, genuinely and truly, some things that you can do to invite passion and substance into your life include:

- Exploring religion. Religion has helped me and so many others find passion in their lives, so of course I have to recommend it to you as well. Even if you don't go with the same religion I practice, religious worship and practice can be one of the most fulfilling ways to find meaning. Not only that, but the community aspect of many religions provides us with an invaluable support group, which is just another amazing benefit.

- Start reading. I know you're reading right now, but try and make it a habit to pick up more books. You don't even have to like reading or books; simply reading exposes us to more aspects of life and passion that we maybe haven't considered, which can be a great way to open doors into inviting more passion into your life.

- Learn a new language. I'm serious—taking a few minutes a day to learn a new language can invite passion and interest into your life, all while teaching yourself a new skill that's useful and tangible.

- Go to a crafts store and pick up a new hobby. Most crafts stores— even the crafting aisle at Walmart—have a plethora of pre-made art kits that you can buy, go home, and engage with a project from. From embroidery to gemstone painting and more, these kits are a wonderful way to invite structured creativity into your life. You might even find a new passion from doing so.

- Go people watching. You might feel weird doing this at first, but there's nothing against sitting down on a park bench with your favorite drink and just... observing. You might be surprised what you can learn about humans from people watching, and it can even invite in unexpected opportunities.

- Go back to school. School is expensive, so I'm not going to say that you should enroll in college right now and get another (or your first) degree. However, utilizing educational tools is a great way to both empower yourself and to find out where new passions lie. If formal schooling isn't an option, websites like Khan Academy and Coursera provide free academic resources that are truly wonderful to explore.

- Try a job change. Again, not possible for everyone, but changing your job if you can provide you with a new touch of scenery that invites new ideas into your life.

- Dedicate every day to trying something new, no matter how small. My last tip for you if you feel like you have no passions is to do something new, no matter how small that thing may be. Maybe you go to a new grocery store for your eggs, or maybe you go skydiving—the world is your oyster and it's up to you to take advantage of that.

I am a strong believer that everyone is passionate about something. Even if you don't know what that passion is, trying things out and setting goals for yourself can be a meaningful way to find purpose while recovering from trauma. But no one should have to do it all alone, which is why we're going to talk about building a support network next!

Building a Support Network

What is a support network? Support networks include friends, family, and other individuals who are trustworthy and willing to be of service in some way when you need them. This can range from being there for you when you're sad to helping you through panic attacks and so much more. Trusting people after trauma is one of the hardest parts of recovery, but it's a part that you need to fight for in order to build support networks and connections that help you flourish into who you are.

There are so many benefits to having a strong support network. For starters, they provide support. If you need something, your support network is always there for you. This also means that you get to be part of that fulfilling exchange and support them as well. In addition, support networks often consist of people who share the same struggles as us. Finding a support network can mean that you receive valuable insights and advice into the recovery process that you might not have had otherwise.

So, what do you do in order to find a support network? You can't just go outside and yell "I need a support network!" after all. Here are a few tips for finding a perfect support network for you:

- Join a support group. There are countless PTSD support groups both in person and online, and these groups are the perfect opportunity to build your support network. People with similar struggles come together to share stories and advice in these groups, which can be exactly what some survivors need.

- Volunteer. Meeting new people as an adult isn't always the easiest thing to do. By picking out a few causes that matter to you and volunteering for them, you have the ability to both make a lasting difference and build your support network.

- Get into contact with old friends, and work to maintain contact with your current ones. PTSD is an isolating experience; if you can, be open and honest about why you've been distant and that you'd like to rekindle connections. Any friends worth keeping around are going to be understanding.

- Use work as an opportunity to network. Most people view work as something to do and then go home, but it can be so much more than that. By attending work events, networking with those you work with, and more, you can connect to a lot of different people—and you might find out that you have more similarities than you think.

- Participate in community events. Every town, no matter how small, has several community events every year. By participating in those events, you get to connect with those around whom you reside and form a local support network that can be truly revolutionary.

I believe that everyone—every soul—is here for a reason, and that includes yours. What that specific meaning turns out to be is for you to figure out, and now you have the tools to do so—congratulations!

Conclusion

PTSD can be one of the most harrowing illnesses to suffer from. An uncanny number of people, myself included, deal with the symptoms of PTSD, including the impact that that has on one's life. While PTSD can be one of the hardest things in the world to manage, you do not have to struggle any longer. Now, you have innumerable tools that allow you to overcome the throes of your PTSD. Just a portion of what you have mastered includes:

- What is PTSD? Understanding not only what PTSD but what causes it and the forms it can come in, as well as how it impacts one's life.

- CBT, DBT, and EMDR therapies: which one is right for you and how do the methods work?

- The role of diet and nutrition on PTSD, and how what you eat and do can encourage the improvement of PTSD symptoms.

- Spiritual solutions for PTSD—everything you need to know about my personal story and how spirituality can transform your PTSD recovery.

- Sleep: why it is so important and how you can achieve the perfect sleep for your needs.

- Self-care for the win—unlock the secrets to self-care, purpose, meaning, and more.

And that's only the half of it. Now, you have so many tangible skills that lead you down the right road for recovery.

Before I leave you to make your own way on this journey, I wanted to thank you. It takes a lot, especially after what you have been through, to trust someone so fully and completely. Thank you so much for allowing me to take you on this transformative journey. It has been just as helpful for me as I hope it has been for you. If you have found this book to be helpful, please leave a review! That way, others can have access to this resource just like you have had, kickstarting their recovery.

So, what are you waiting for? Take what you have gathered from this resource and go live your best life—one where you control your PTSD and *not* the other way around. I believe in you.

Leaving a Review

One-Click Review!

I truly hope you enjoyed "PTSD Solutions" and that one (or more) of the solutions that worked for me will work for you too! Reviews are SO very important. I would be incredibly thankful if you would please take less than 1 minute to leave a rating/review by clicking or visiting:

https://www.amazon.com/review/create-review?&asin=B0BWL8LGY4

If you read a print version, please type the address listed above into your internet browser to be sent directly to the review page for this book (also can go back to the Amazon purchase page, click on "ratings", and then "leave a review"). Thank you in advance for your time and support!

Thank you!

References

8 Self-Care Tips To Manage Stress. (2013, November 24). Psych Central. https://psychcentral.com/stress/practicing-self-care-during-stressful-times

Australia, H. (2023, May 24). *Exercise and mental health.* Www.healthdirect.gov.au. https://www.healthdirect.gov.au/exercise-and-mental-health#:~:text=Exercise%20causes%20your%20brain%20to

Brainline. (2018, February 22). *DSM-5 Criteria for PTSD.* BrainLine. https://www.brainline.org/article/dsm-5-criteria-ptsd

Can We Inherit PTSD from Our Parents? | Genetics And Genomics. (n.d.). LabRoots. https://www.labroots.com/trending/genetics-and-genomics/14979/inherit-ptsd-parents

Cleveland Clinic. (2022, August 4). *Cognitive Behavioral Therapy (CBT).* Cleveland Clinic. https://my.clevelandclinic.org/health/treatments/21208-cognitive-behavioral-therapy-cbt

Cooks-Campbell, A. (2022, July 15). *Triggers: Learn to Recognize and Deal With Them.* BetterUp. https://www.betterup.com/blog/triggers

Eating Well for Mental Health | Sutter Health. (n.d.). Www.sutterhealth.org. https://www.sutterhealth.org/health/nutrition/eating-well-for-mental-health#:~:text=What%20we

EMDR Therapy: What It Is, Procedure & Effectiveness. (n.d.). Cleveland Clinic. Retrieved June 19, 2023, from https://my.clevelandclinic.org/health/treatments/22641-emdr-therapy#:~:text=Dozens%20of%20studies%20have%20found

Experiencing EMDR Therapy. (n.d.). EMDR International Association. https://www.emdria.org/about-emdr-therapy/experiencing-emdr-therapy/

Exposure Therapy for Anxiety: What to Expect and Effectiveness. (2021, June 10). Healthline. https://www.healthline.com/health/anxiety/exposure-therapy-for-anxiety#:~:text=How%20effective%20is%20it%3F

Exposure therapy: What it is and what to expect. (2020, May 5). Www.medicalnewstoday.com. https://www.medicalnewstoday.com/articles/exposure-therapy#What-to-expect

Hartney, E. (2020, November 30). *10 Cognitive Distortions That Can Lead to Addiction Relapse.* Verywell Mind. https://www.verywellmind.com/ten-cognitive-distortions-identified-in-cbt-22412

How Post Traumatic Stress Disorder Affects Sleep. (2020, September 18). Sleep Foundation. https://www.sleepfoundation.org/mental-health/ptsd-and-sleep#:~:text=causes%20sleep%20problems.-

Mind. (2021a, January). *Causes of PTSD.* Www.mind.org.uk. https://www.mind.org.uk/information-support/types-of-mental-health-problems/post-traumatic-stress-disorder-ptsd-and-complex-ptsd/causes/

Mind. (2021b, January). *What is complex PTSD?* Www.mind.org.uk. https://www.mind.org.uk/information-support/types-of-mental-health-problems/post-traumatic-stress-disorder-ptsd-and-complex-ptsd/complex-ptsd/

NHS. (2021). *Symptoms - Post-traumatic stress disorder.* Nhs.uk. https://www.nhs.uk/mental-health/conditions/post-traumatic-stress-disorder-ptsd/symptoms/

Night terrors and nightmares. (2017, October 25). Nhs.uk. https://www.nhs.uk/conditions/night-terrors/#:~:text=Night%20terrors%20and%20nightmares%20are

Office, C. A. O. (n.d.). *Developing healthy coping skills for resilience.* Hr.wustl.edu. https://hr.wustl.edu/developing-healthy-coping-skills-for-resilience/#:~:text=Psychologists%20have%20identified%20four%20key

Pedersen, T. (2022, April 28). *Triggers: What They Are, How They Form, and What to Do.* Psych Central. https://psychcentral.com/lib/what-is-a-trigger

Shapiro, F. (2014). The Role of Eye Movement Desensitization and Reprocessing (EMDR) Therapy in Medicine: Addressing the Psychological and Physical Symptoms Stemming from Adverse Life Experience. *The Permanente Journal*, *18*(1), 71–77. https://doi.org/10.7812/tpp/13-098

Spirituality and Healing. (2015, January 14). Hms.harvard.edu. https://hms.harvard.edu/news/spirituality-healing#:~:text=Belief%20in%20a%20deity%20engenders

VA.gov | Veterans Affairs. (n.d.). Www.ptsd.va.gov. https://www.ptsd.va.gov/family/effect_relationships.asp#:~:text=Social%20support%20is%20one%20of

Printed in Great Britain
by Amazon

39364167R00059